Where We Lived

ESSAYS ON PLACES

D1320435

Other Books by Henry Allen

Fool's Mercy, a novel

Going Too Far Enough: American Culture at Century's End

The Museum of Lost Air, poetry

What It Felt Like: Living in the American Century

Where We Lived

ESSAYS ON PLACES

Henry Allen

MANDEL VILAR PRESS / DRYAD PRESS

Copyright © 2017 by Henry Allen.
All rights reserved. Printed in the United States.

Book and cover design by Sandy Rodgers.
Cover Art by Henry Allen.

Acknowledgments
Some of these chapters have appeared in altered form in *The New Yorker*, *Military History*, *The Washington Post*, and the *Hamilton College Spectator*.

Published by
Mandel Vilar Press / www.mvpress.org
19 Oxford Court, Simsbury, Connecticut 06070

Dryad Press / www.dryadpress.com
15 Sherman Avenue, Takoma Park, Maryland 20912

Library of Congress Cataloging-in-Publication Data

Names: Allen, Henry, author.
Title: Where we lived : essays on places / Henry Allen.
Description: First American paperback edition. | Simsbury, Connecticut :
 Mandel Vilar Press ; Takoma Park, Maryland : Dryad Press, 2017.
Identifiers: LCCN 2017027988 (print) | LCCN 2017038524 (ebook) | ISBN
 9781942134459 | ISBN 9781942134442 (paperback)
Subjects: LCSH: Allen, Henry--Homes and haunts. | Allen, Henry--Family. |
 Home. | Family. | Life change events. | BISAC: HISTORY / Social History.
Classification: LCC PS3501.L4995 (ebook) | LCC PS3501.L4995 A6 2017 (print) |
 DDC 814/.54 [B] --dc23
LC record available at https://lccn.loc.gov/2017027988

To all of them, ancestors and scions, dead, alive and yet to be born, who made this book not only possible but imperative. And to all the other unrelated people who did the same — their love and encouragement bewilders me but I accept it because clearly they know something I don't.

Contents

Foreword

This book is a curiosity, notes jotted in a sickbed, a telegram to my children and my grandchildren, an outburst of passion in a time of calm and golf.

It is family history but it is not the sort of history that is milled to the fineness of fourth cousins, or a dusty heap of collateral celebrities of which there are some in my family — John Winthrop, Robert Fulton, Samuel Colt. If your family arrived in New England long ago, you're related to enough notable names to stock an academic index.

But they will not appear here. Instead, this book is an oddity, the sort of thing you might find on a rainy day in a summer house when you jimmy the owner's closet and find a manuscript. You read it on the porch, in the coziness of rain dripping off pine trees. You wonder why it was written at all. It is so private it makes you feel like an intruder.

"What are you reading?" your daughter asks, looking at

the pages scattered around you along with an afternoon's worth of tea bags.

"It's about the family that used to own this house," you say.

She looks. She wrinkles her nose. She squints. She drops the pages next to your mug of tea.

"Are we going to the inn for dinner?" she asks. She doesn't care. That's fine. This has not been written for her — or for you, however kind or curious you are to be reading this.

It's as if I feared my children and their children would never know about the lost worlds of our family — love, moral stands, disappointment, Christmas dinners, the ancient and ordinary sunlight that transported us like aliens from galaxies of the past. These galaxies not only existed but persisted despite the apathy of their inheritors. Consider this book a last will and testament, an attempt to stave off the probate of oblivion.

Where We Lived

ESSAYS ON PLACES

Grandfather Harry Allen at 407 Highland Ave.

407 Highland Ave.

. . . a wing chair smelling of the insides of hats . . .

In the early 1950s, my grandfather, Harry Allen, sold the family house in Orange, N.J.

It was the sensible thing to do. My grandmother was long dead, their three sons were gone. It was an old ark of a place, as my mother would say. Its time was over.

Nevertheless, even as postwar America levitated into television modernity and Cold War paranoia, it would linger as a sense of foreclosed possibility, of diaspora. It was like a planet that disappears, leaving only its gravity behind.

Not that losing it was a tragedy — more a case of Olympian wistfulness, and the old truth that we have to change or pay more to stay the same. Still, there was something heroic about life there, heroically modest in the vanishing style that sought the respect of friends but not the envy of rivals.

It was called 407 after its address, 407 Highland Ave., an early Victorian, a big house on a street of big houses. It had high ceilings — airy and claustrophobic at the same time, like a church. It had a cured smell, the comfortable pungence of a can of pipe tobacco or mink coats in closets. There were huge Oriental rugs, wingback chairs and stand-up ashtrays. On tables were crystal, bronze, and sterling silver with monograms — cigarette boxes, porringers, picture frames and a tea set of architectural splendor. To me, at 10 or so, it all had the air of furnishings for a ritual, however outworn.

My grandfather, Henry Southworth Allen, Jr., called Harry, was a managing partner at Spencer Trask, a Wall Street investment bank, a station in life that gave him much satisfaction. He bought 407 after World War I. An artist had owned it once. He had added a studio that went up two stories, leaving exterior bedroom windows overlooking what became the living room. After bedtime, we children could peer down on the mystery of grownups in their own world, the men backhanding logs into the fireplace and lighting the women's cigarettes.

When the three Allen sons — my father the eldest, the namesake — got together there on holidays they had wary smiles, as if life at 407 were an inside joke. They had grace,

too, gliding around in pleated trousers that hung from high 1940s waists. They lightly hitched them up by the creases before they sat down. They held cigarettes at the last knuckle of their fingers and smoked only half of them. They had spent their youths on the right lists — coming-out parties at the Ritz-Carlton and the Plaza. That was before the war.

By my time, the old Anglo-Saxon stock was losing sway. The grace of my father's world had given way to power, though he retained the best and easiest manners of any man I have known. They accompanied his belief that "everything comes back."

The Allen sons' wives wore wide-shouldered dresses with narrow waists and they braced their elbows against their ribs to hold cigarettes up like devil-may-care torches. They all seemed to be leaning slightly backwards. They seemed resigned — they'd been married long enough to suspect that the Allen boys would disappoint them, sons of a father who'd raised them to have the off-handed demeanor of the rich he admired. It was the money that was the problem.

There had been money at 407 but in 1931 one of my grandfather's partners made a catastrophic deal on Canadian timber and soon my grandmother, Mildred, made her legendary vow: "The next time we've got money like that, we're

17

going to spend a little of it." In photographs she has a bold, open face. I have one of her at the tiller of an electric car — she was said to be the second licensed woman driver in Massachusetts. She came from New Bedford. Much of her family's textile money had been lost when "the mills went South," as my father would say, with an oddly formal mournfulness.

As a young woman, my mother had played cards with her in the front room. She thought the middle-aged meander of veins on the backs of Mil's hands was beautiful. Along with the grand piano, which had chipped keys and a heavy action, there was a radio. On Saturday afternoons in the 1930s, my father and his mother used to listen to the Metropolitan Opera together. The Christmas tree went next to the piano. In my time, I had the feeling it had been decorated by the maids, Rose and Pauline, and nobody had looked at it.

Rose and Pauline had also become the cooks after the Depression foreclosed on certain possibilities — Packards, a water view summerhouse in Southport, Conn., a cook.

Their kitchen had an industrial feeling — only servants used it, after all. I remember a smell of hominy. An old cookie jar stood on a counter but there were never any cookies in it. There was a back staircase I liked, an invitation to rainy day playfulness while the rest of the house seemed to constrain that sort of thing. There was a big hole in the pantry door.

"Rats," my father explained. I wonder now why it hadn't been patched.

When Fanny came to do the laundry there was a thick sharp smell of soap and steam. All three women were black. Fanny had put her son through medical school and then he lost his medical license for performing abortions. "It broke her heart," my father said — he cared most for people as individuals rather than social abstractions, though he voted for Roosevelt and the New Deal, perhaps in secret. His father called him "Ruse-evelt" in the manner of Republicans who hated him.

Despite financial setbacks the Allens of 407 were still rich by most reckonings but like F. Scott Fitzgerald they knew the vast distance between the rich and the very rich, the ones who are different from you and me.

One asset held firm: the proprietary air that lurks in families who arrived in New England in the first half of the 1600s. We were descendants of the Old Ones, the God-bitten Indian killers of New England whose descendants would have presidents to dinner, and whose ghosts still haunted multi-poly-diversity America. This heritage was seldom mentioned, and then only with a tone of voice meant to dismiss it as irrelevant. Anything more would have seemed immodest and undemocratic.

Henry Southworth Allen, III.

My father, the third Henry Southworth Allen (I am the fourth) was born in 1910. He grew up in a world of knickers, coal furnaces, servants, trolley cars, neckties worn on golf courses, and the Jazz Age of Fitzgerald, whom he disdained for flamboyance unbecoming a fellow Princeton man.

In photographs he has the presumptuous earnestness of a boarding school boy (St. George's, 1928) and a slight hardness to his stare, the sort of look that military officers cultivate. He was proud of his boyhood, and he wanted me to have a boyhood like it, busy with hobbies, experiments, and collections. I disappointed him.

He played the piano in the front room. He could play the easier Chopin but his first love was musical comedy. He bought sheet music and learned the American songbook as it was being written. He taught himself to draw. He collected stamps his father brought home from his office at Spencer Trask, stamps from now-vanished countries — Abyssinia, the Dutch East Indies. He listened to a crystal-set radio. He read St. Nicholas magazine for children with its stories by authors with three names such as Albert Payson Terhune, who wrote about dogs.

Dad had a dog, a Boston bull terrier named Bobby. When I was a boy after World War II he took me into the back yard of 407 and showed me where he had buried Bobby.

"I put his collar on the fencepost," he said, his face going simple with grief.

"What happened to the collar?" I asked.

He startled me by snapping: "That rotted away years ago."

My grandmother died at 56 of asthma and heart disease just after I was born in 1941. She and her death seemed to occupy 407 just out of peripheral vision. My grandfather took refuge in a small, dark, ground-floor bedroom. He would lead my younger sister Julie and me in there, lift us up and let us put one hand in his penny jar. We could keep all the pennies we could hold, a lesson in the fundamentals of capitalism.

He had a little potbelly and quick eyes, a busy precision about him — in middle age he learned to figure skate in the old style, gliding backward to draw figure eights.

He believed in homeopathy. He was superstitious. If he saw a man on crutches during his morning ferry ride to Wall Street and then the market went down, he'd come home grumbling about the "goddam cripple." After very bad days, he would throw away the necktie he'd worn.

Into the 1940s he still went to New York on Saturdays to work a half day in the old style. He would not return until evening. My father asked him once what he did with the other half of the day.

He said: "I have lunch with Kerensky and then we go antique shopping."

Kerensky! Alexander Kerensky, who lived in New York then, had been prime minister of Russia, the last chance for democracy before the Bolsheviks overthrew him. I love the bravado of this lie. The truth was, my grandfather spent Saturdays with his secretary and their son — he had another family.

I wrote a poem about this.

Grandpa had a mistress.
The mistress had a son.

When Grandpa died the cancelled checks
Would show what he had done.

He was everything to my father. My mother despised him.
"He was such a phony," she would say.

She resented him for allowing one and only one martini
to be served before dinner. He kept a close eye on the drinking, a family disease.

I suspect my mother resented having to fight him for my
father's loyalty. He insisted that my father — though not his
younger brother, David — follow him to Wall Street as if it
were a family legacy. My grandmother thought he should
be an Episcopal priest, but she was overruled. I think he
would have found the
clergy tedious, but he
found working as a bond
broker tedious too — and
he lacked the knack for
making money. As for my
father's own youthful
ambitions, he mooned

*Grandmother and her sons, Peter,
Henry, III, and David, 1926.*

over two impossible romances: Broadway songwriting and
the sea as he read about it in Joseph Conrad.

Through family connections Dad went to sea as a merchant sailor during summers at Princeton, to Brazil and to China. At Princeton he tried out for the Triangle Club, whose celebrated musical show used to tour from city to city every year. My father's year, Jimmy Stewart made it but Dad and his songs were turned down. I think he was crushed — it was a foreclosure. He kept writing songs, though. He thought his best was one called "Winter Coming On."

> So here am I
> With nothing to do but sigh
> in the long night, the lonely night
> of winter coming on.

Near the end of his junior year, he quit Princeton to attempt a trans-Atlantic sail in a 36-foot Friendship sloop with two friends — a feat so daring then that it was covered in at least one New York newspaper. The boat sprung a board 500 miles out and they had to pump their way back to Nova Scotia where my father got a job harpooning swordfish while repairs were made. He hated killing the swordfish, the cruelty of it.

He told me about his boyhood failures, perhaps to comfort me for mine. Once at his boarding school, St. George's, he was running down a football field with the winning pass arcing toward him. I thought he'd tell me he won the game but instead, he said, he dropped the ball. I was sorry he told me.

In Southport, before the Depression, my father crewed on a Star boat that tied for first in the Eastern championships. The skipper had already rented a flatcar to haul the boat to San Francisco for the Nationals. In the sail-off, the other Star went out looking for wind on a reach and found it, and that was that.

So many almosts, so many not quites.

My grandfather's proprieties wore down my grandmother — she also had to deal with Harry's mother and his unmarried sister Florrie, who also lived at 407 and took his side.

Mil got her revenge, though, when her youngest son, Peter, was born in 1922. She "spoiled him rotten," my mother would say with satisfaction. He was a wild child who saw the family's decorum as a joke, not an obligation. At three, the legend had it, he ran crying into the house: "Goddam bee stung me."

He would go on to a series of school expulsions and car wrecks — after one he awoke in a Catholic hospital, saw the winged cornettes of the Sisters of Charity and thought he was in heaven, watched over by angels. There were gambling debts, a teenage elopement, and lost jobs. He was also a war hero decorated for risking his life to put out a fire in his B-24 over Europe. He was the smartest son and the funniest, the black sheep we all loved. We named our first son after him.

I knew from family stories that there had been much fun at 407. At the dinner table on festive occasions, they would put napkins on their heads and say to each other in turn, "This is a very serious occasion" until they were laughing too hard to continue. Thanksgiving visitors were subjected to the mince pie prank, about how lucky they were to have mince pie that year.

"Really, Mr. Allen?"

"You haven't heard about the mince blight? It was in all the papers."

"Oh, I'd always thought mince was made from lots of things chopped up."

"Many people do, but it grows in bogs."

"Like cranberries? "

"Much like cranberries."

They might go on to discuss investments in mince futures, mince fortunes made and lost, and so on until the guest caught on. On holidays, the best part of dinner for me was the desserts Rose and Pauline made with brandy — pies and hard sauce. The alcohol fumes were supposed to catch fire but despite the lighting of many matches, flames were fugitive.

Rose and Pauline stayed on until 407 was sold. By that time, there was a new suburban way of life that excluded servants and the fixed schedules that went with them. On Sundays, for instance, they had gone to early church, and then cooked Sunday dinner for the family to eat when they returned from the 11 o'clock service.

My parents tried but failed to keep Sunday dinner alive in our little postwar house one county over from 407. While my mother cooked it, my sister and I had to wait in our church clothes, knowing our friends were outside playing.

Grandpa visited us but he looked uncomfortable in our house and complained of drafts.

His beloved Wall Street had lost prestige in the Depression and the New Deal.

In 1938, my father was on the floor of the Stock Exchange when the bell rang to stop trading, a rare and drastic event. There was an announcement. Richard Whitney, former president of the Exchange, treasurer of the New York Yacht Club, master of the Far Hills Hunt and the model of everything admired at 407 had been arrested. The crime was the sleaziest of betrayals on Wall Street then — embezzlement from funds he oversaw.

"Richard Whitney!" my father said to me. "Richard Whitney! Impossible!" It was reported that people crowded Grand Central Station to see him taken off to prison in handcuffs.

After commanding a landing ship through the carnage at Okinawa and satisfying any craving he still had for the sea, my father defied my grandfather and quit Wall Street to sell wholesale silverware. He liked selling. He was good at it, though later he was not as good when he moved into management. Grandpa insisted that he describe himself not as a salesman but as a "district sales manager." Meanwhile, my uncles lived as if they were in exile, moving through futureless jobs and out-of-the-way cities. David ran an Eastern Airlines ticket office in Atlantic City, I remember, and Peter moved from rental to rental, one step ahead of the landlord.

Whiskey, the sovereign remedy for the pain of change, became a way of living that was also a way of dying, a borrowing against a future that never comes. Instead there came business disappointments, debts, and marrying down, a regression to the mean. Along with his boyhood, the Navy was my father's greatest success.

Its hat factories long gone, Orange was turning shabby. Before the tracks were torn up my grandfather took me for a ride so I'd know what a trolley had been — family legend had it that as a stunt, a distant cousin had travelled from New Jersey to Rhode Island on the interurban trolley that once linked towns on the East Coast.

With stunning crassness or encroaching dementia, my grandfather remarried in a grand church wedding with flower girls, the flinging of rose petals and a celebrity minister, Dr. Norman Vincent Peale, author of "The Power of Positive Thinking." The new wife, named Molly, turned out to be a drunk and a hanger-on of ministers who bilked her and us. My mother said she gave 407's Oriental rugs — and who knows what else — to someone she called "the Revender Cooper."

In a last chance for 407, my grandfather offered to sell it to my father, but he or my mother or both of them said no. I liked the idea — my last chance at equaling my father's boyhood — but I recall them saying it would cost a fortune to heat. Saying no was the sensible thing to do.

Grandpa and Molly moved to a stuffy apartment in a building my father called "Menopause Hall." Grandpa died there during a nap after church on Easter Sunday. My sister and I were not taken to the funeral. I don't know why. I wonder now if the mistress and her son, our half-uncle, were there.

The widow pestered my father with drunken late-night phone calls. She stepped in a paint pot and fell downstairs. We heard she'd gone into a nursing home and then we lost track of her. I think my father felt she was the living corruption of everything that 407 and his mother had stood for. In a burst of cynicism he said his father had married her because he thought she had money.

407 HIGHLAND AVE., ORANGE, N.J.

When I think of my grandfather's house I think
of my father looking pointedly serene
in a boarding school photograph
by the standup ashtray that squeaked
in the giant living room that huddled
under the brown and possible dusks
of northern New Jersey, everything feeling
safe and doomed at the same time in 1947. I also think:
of a wing chair smelling of the insides of hats,
of my grandmother, who was always dead,
of headaches in the mirrors,

of daughters-in-law desperate in the powder room, and
of a grand piano that smelled like old, old Christmas trees
    and chuckled and thumped between the keys
of boyhood songs my father played just parts of,
    ill at ease.
I think of a kitchen that smelled of hominy and steam —
    so did the maids, Rose and Pauline. I think
of Aunt Florry who smelled like tongue depressors,
and died on Easter weekend, buying cookies
    for my sister and me.
    Right in the bakery,
    right on the floor.
    I'll never eat cookies
    on Easter anymore.
I think of 1929 in the radio,
of Kerensky in the martini glasses,
of fury in the Sunday roast,
of truth in the kick under the table,
of the flame that wandered sluggish
    o'er the Christmas pudding,
of a green fluid in a glass swan barometer,
of funny Uncle Peter and puzzled Uncle David,
of the Allen boys' tuxedos in trolley cars
and how everything happened Before the War,

and especially I think
of Grandpa who smelled like damp foreheads,
   and was smart;
of Grandpa having a mistress,
   and the mistress a son —
   when Grandpa died the cancelled checks
   would show what he had done;
I think of Our Kind of People,
and how That's Not The Way We Do Things In This Family;
I think how nothing was permitted,
but Everything Was Real;
and of my mother, mean as a scared child,
eating her soup at those holiday dinners.
But mostly I think of my father,
   with his face like a lottery ticket,
   with his face like shined shoes
   lined up in a closet,
of my father's smile waiting for the shutter to click,
of his smile pinned to me like a medal for deeds I didn't do,
of years later, and the big, tired shoulders
   of a skinny man gone fat,
of the terrible wisdom of his face under hospital stubble.

Now I am the oldest man in the family. I have lived my
life in the exile of bohemia and journalism. After claiming

some casualties, the family disease is finally in remission —
I haven't had a drink for more than 20 years. There are great-
grandchildren and great-great-grandchildren with newfound energy and delight in life — from a law partner, a
school principal and a ski champion to a four-year-old in a
tutu on Halloween. This chronicle will mean little to them
— history stops at your grandparents. And when my sister
and I die, along with a few cousins, there will be no one to
remember our 407, no one to honor its tutelary deities, which
is to say there will be no 407 at all by our lights, just an old
house in an exhausted city in New Jersey.

Farmhouse in Wales bought by a family ancestor in 1557.

Starting in 1557

. . . rivers of the windfall light . . .

t is a summer-day photograph — white house on a gentle hill in Wales and behind it black trees against the sky. There are white geese, black chickens and four farmhands waiting for the picture to be taken.

Inside I imagine a dim ramble of uneven stone floors, cool plaster walls and sills scalloped by age, all of it inhabited by an ancient tang of soured milk, dogs, diapers and kidney pies. Most of the house probably dates from after Griffith ap Owen bought the place in 1557 — 13 generations before me and also called Gruffud ap Owen and Griffith Bowen). All that may be left from his house, I have read, are a door with freestone jambs and a freestone arch that once led to a dairy. I have never been there. Except as a genealogical curiosity, it arouses no sentiment of the sort that inspired Dylan Thomas to write his best poem, "Fern

Hill," about a farm he knew while growing up in nearby Swansea.

> And once below a time I lordly had the trees and leaves
> Trail with daisies and barley
> Down the rivers of the windfall light.

I see no windfall light in the photograph, just the glare of another noon among centuries of farmhouse noons. The house is a bluff forehead of a place, all business.

This is the oldest family house I've found though I haven't looked any further than a book on a shelf three feet behind me, a privately printed family history from 1930, the sort that New England families began to write in the 19th century when they saw their money and hegemony dwindling. They reckoned that their one unchallengeable possession was their lineage, with particular interest paid to their history since their arrival in wilderness Massachusetts. Somehow this arrival conferred on them an importance they had not had as middle-class religious fanatics in Britain.

They prospered in New England, and the most prosperous of them would become aristocrats. After a while they came to believe that their wealth was the result of their "good breeding" rather than the cause of it. One didn't make money, one had money. Their Calvinist beliefs made it easy for them to believe that their fortunes were a sign of God's grace, rather than the work and luck of their forebears. The aristocracy thereby turned into a caste, as aristocracies do, with entitlements rather than achievements, privileges instead of obligations. People of this sort don't do, they just are.

Then the money seeps away, getting halved in divorces and divided among heirs. The land is sold off to save the house, and then the house is sold because no one wants to live there. After many arguments about rotting roofs and sagging porches, the summer place gets sold too. Sons become chefs and carpenters, the daughters marry down. Just as surely as distinguished breeding begins with money, it can end in poverty. I'm sure that tarpaper backwoods snowmobile New England has more than a few distant cousins of mine floating face down in the shallow end of the gene pool.

Griffith Bowen's great-grandson, also called Griffith Bowen, emigrated from Wales to Boston in 1638 with his wife, Margaret Fleming, and five children. He built a house at the corner of Washington and Essex streets, a block from Boston Common. He had four more children. I imagine all those feet echoing off plank floors and low, hewn-beam ceilings. I picture the old-country furniture they brought with them, poignantly ornate in the new world of work and wilderness. Griffith Bowen farmed 150 acres in Brookline. After about 11 years of pulling stumps, clearing fields, and staggering under the weight of rocks piled to form stone walls — or whatever labors he and his sons performed, all watched over by the sharp, decided eyes of Puritan elders and Indians — he went back to Britain and died there.

He left behind children, some of whom moved from Boston to Woodstock, Conn. where they would build their own houses and be farmers, bishops, and ambassadors.

A Bowen fought at Bunker Hill. Another, a surgeon with Custer's 7th Cavalry, was killed at Little Big Horn. Henry Chandler Bowen, a rich merchant and publisher of an abolitionist newspaper, *The New York Independent*, built a pink Gothic Revival summer house in Woodstock, called Roseland. Four presidents are said to have visited it. A family history describes President Grant exiled to a porch to smoke his cigars and drink his whiskey, both forbidden by Henry inside the house. It still stands. (I saw it when I took my father's ashes to Woodstock in 1982, and spread them in a pond given to the town by the Bowens.)

Only a few decades after the glory days of Roseland (or the Pink House, as we called it) my branch of the Bowen family lost its money when New Bedford's textile mills went South for cheaper labor and my great-grandfather Bowen repurposed himself as a drinker. Toward

The pink house.

the end of his life he moved to Orange, N.J. to live with my grandparents — his daughter, Mildred Bowen Allen, and my grandfather Harry.

On my grandfather Harry Allen's side, Bristol, R.I., is still thickly settled by a family descended from the piratical DeWolfs, a rough and money-hungry bunch. They owned a plantation on Guadeloupe, they owned mills in Old Lyme, Conn. On March 5, 1656, the founder of the North American line, Balthazar DeWolf, was hauled into a Hartford court "for smoking in the streets contra to the law." It is said in a family annal that "he paid his fine, lit his pipe, and walked out." He moved to the Connecticut coast in the Saybrook area. Though he had chafed under Puritanical restrictions he was known as a "witch hunter." He took part in the trial of one Nicholas Jennings, who was said to have bewitched one of Balthazar's sons to death. "The jury hung and Jennings escaped the gallows, though not the suspicions of his fellow Puritans."

Balthazar and his son Edward fought in the bloody King Philip's War in 1675-76, and were said to be "in at the kill" of King Philip, a Wampanoag chief also known as Massasoit. Edward died in 1712, and his grave is still decorated every Memorial Day with a veteran's American flag.

The Rhode Island branch of the DeWolfs began when Mark Anthony DeWolf of Guadeloupe, married the sister of Simeon Potter, a privateer from Bristol.

Potter is remembered for saying: "Get money, get money. I would plow the seas for oat porridge if I could but get money."

Given this philosophy, the DeWolfs had a knack for both making fortunes and losing them. General George DeWolf, a slaver and a gunrunner, borrowed from enough of the townspeople that a mob stormed his mansion, ripping down the damask curtains and leaving it an empty shell after they learned he'd absconded to the Caribbean with their money. The most famous DeWolf, James, known as "Captain Jim," may have been the biggest transporter of slaves in American history. He had a fleet larger than the U.S. Navy. He was tried twice for murder after he tied a female slave with smallpox to a chair and threw her overboard to keep her from infecting the rest of the ship. He was not convicted. He would become a United States senator after amassing the second largest fortune in America according to a plaque in the Hope Street mansion, now called Linden Place.

It is a big wedding cake of a house, a carbuncle of elegance amid Puritan modesty, a monitor-on-hip-roof Federal with a two-story, four-columned Corinthian portico. Andrew Jackson dined there. Later, the actress Ethel Barrymore spent summers there during a brief marriage. Now tourists pay to go through it, and the house is rented out for weddings. In its heyday, I imagine a busy, bookless place where hardened men were always just back from a voyage or about to embark on one, and the women's souls

The wedding cake of a house.

grew calloused amid the gaudiness and hard dealing. Get money, get money.

I descend from James's younger brother, Levi. He did not get money. He made one trip to Africa and refused to make more, thereby forswearing a fortune. He was said to be pious. In 1793 he built a clapboard box of a New England farmhouse a mile or so up Hope Street from Linden Place. There is a pedimented front door but the house is charmless, still possessing a preoccupied farmhouse utility, a little shabby now, the farm long gone. He filled it with children, one of whom, Mary, married Samuel Sterling Allen, who may have come from a family in Warren, R.I.

They produced Mark Anthony DeWolf Allen, father of Henry Southworth Allen, whose name I bear with the numeral IV at the end.

He lived with my grandparents too, dying when my father was 8. He was cited in an obituary as a "chemical salesman." I have seen no photographs of him. All my father ever said about him was that he was "just a real nice guy." His wife, my great-grandmother, was said to be a shrew. When the boys played too close to the house she'd rap on a windowpane with her ring to tell them to stop.

I suppose a scouring of records might reveal deed trans-

fers or children who died in infancy, brides' books, letters
with mentions of long-vanished souvenir teaspoons. But
unless you're the family genealogist who obsesses about
these things, you wouldn't bother. Despite the untellable
vastness of their souls on earth, these people are gone. As
we say nowadays when we dismiss people, they are history,
by which we mean vanished, irrelevant, inconsequential,
trivial, not worth our attention.

Someday it will be our turn to evaporate like moon jel-
lyfish stranded on a sunny beach. Only our memories or
imaginations keep the past alive, and they do such a sloppy
job of it. Then they vanish too. If the Greeks' heaven was
lasting fame, it's a place with the approximate population
density of Greenland.

Still, if you feel a small and antique electricity vibrating
in your bones, little aftershocks from the earthquake of old
existences, you may find some honor in remembering these
people.

The Hindenburg *just after my father saw it glide over Manhattan.*

Salad Days

. . . The ghostly majesty of hydrogen . . .

At my wintry age, how do I remember that before I was born my parents' building superintendent was named Willie Yarosh? How do I have such solid images of their salad days in New York apartments? They told me about them and for some reason I found them important enough to remember.

"We scrimped and saved but we made do," as my mother would say. One might assume a succession of cold-water flats after their wedding in 1935, but in fact their apartments were in Brooklyn Heights and Manhattan's Sutton Place.

Such fun with other salad days couples, by their telling — the husbands just out of law school or moving into their father's companies and my father trading bonds on the New York Stock Exchange. They had parties. They drank complicated cocktails like Old Fashioneds, with sugar, Angostura bitters and a piece of fruit. My father had a piano and my parents' friends in neckties and pearls would stand around it holding drinks and cigarettes, and singing. Everyone knew the college songs: Princeton's "Old Nassau," Yale's "Whiffenpoof Song," or the rousing "Lord Jeffrey Amherst." And the World War I songs: "Mademoiselle from Armentieres," "Over There," "K-K-K-Katy."

I see my mother intense and awkward in front of a stove for the first time in her life, one day calling the fire department to put out a grease fire. From his days harpooning swordfish in Nova Scotia, my father once cooked a fisherman's stew called slumgullion, and everyone who ate it got instant fevers. Why do I remember this?

Friends tell me I have a remarkable memory. I reply with crushing modesty that it just seems that way because I do all the talking. My memory has its oddities, I'll admit — I can remember the casts of movies I've never seen — this morning, it was Betty Hutton and Howard Keel in 1950s *Annie Get Your Gun*. In high school I could quote months-old conversations with girls I loved, word for word.

Memory has never seemed like memory to me — until recently, everything in my life existed in a present that felt no more than a day ago, still malleable, good for a do-over. As Gatsby said: "Can't repeat the past? Of course you can." When I recalled embarrassments from half a century ago, redemption by apology or explanation seemed just a phone call away, a phone call I never made, let me add.

Only now do I recall a past so strange and obliquely contingent that it seems irretrievable, and so I've decided to store it here as if by cryogenics, the idea being that someday it could be thawed and revived.

On the afternoon of May 6, 1937, a Thursday, my father stood on the Sutton Place roof to watch the pride of Hitler's Germany, the dirigible Hindenburg, float with the ghostly majesty of hydrogen down the length of Manhattan. "You could see the swastikas on the fins," he said.

Hours later, while mooring at Lakehurst, New Jersey, the Hindenburg's hydrogen exploded, the frame collapsed and the age of the hydrogen dirigible was over. Of the 97 people on board, 35 died. The dramatic explosion and fire, captured on the new medium of film and broadcast nationally, was written into the national psyche, a catastrophe remembered forever like the sinking of the *Titanic* and later the explosion of the space shuttle *Challenger* or the terrorist destruction of the World Trade Center by hijacked airplanes.

I learned about my father and the Hindenburg from his journal. I saw the journal once for about an hour in the 1970s. He had kept it from the salad days till 1943 when he went off to war. By then, my parents were living in New Providence, New Jersey. They and their best friends in New York, Bob and Peggy Fay, bought neighboring houses that backed up on woods in the Watchung mountains, rural enough that they'd have fun shooting at cans with a single-shot Winchester .22 rifle that sits now, lightly oiled, in a closet next to my studio. The two families, the Allens and the Fays, had their children while living in those houses.

It was all in the journal, a stack of black-and-white school notebooks holding my father's angled and masculine handwriting. I found them in my 40s, by accident in an apartment in New Haven. How had I, the boy spy, historian and rainy-day ransacker of bureau drawers and attics, finder of love letters, never known they existed? I read as much as I could in one sitting, never imagining it would be my only chance, that they would throw them away when they auctioned off their books, their furniture, everything that drew a bid.

The Hindenburg. The Communists marching down Wall

Street shaking their fists and chanting "Bread! Bread!" The night in 1938 my father put on his white tie and tails and took my mother to hear the legendary jazz concert by Benny Goodman and his Orchestra — jazz daring to venture into the sacred precincts of Carnegie Hall. The band played way above itself that night, still a miracle to hear. A recording includes the crowd erupting in amazed applause. I like knowing that my parents' clapping is part of it.

My father had continued his journal by sending my mother letters chronicling the battle of Okinawa as fought on the *LCI 1091*, a 158-foot ship he skippered through months of horror — kamikazes, 30 American ships sunk, 5000 American sailors killed. To his astonished disappointment when he got back, she told him she had thrown those letters away. On her part, she rarely wrote to him, he told me.

She seemed to resent his war and the world of men — she had grown up with a brilliant and athletic father given to terrifying his daughters by getting drunk and pounding the dinner table. She escaped him by quitting Barnard and marrying my father at 18.

After the war he may have missed the world of men. He joined a softball league in our new town of Fanwood, N.J.

One afternoon my mother and I watched from the bleachers. I liked seeing him out there with the guys, the back and forth. But my mother's face went dark and hard — she resented something there.

Much later she threw away my father's uniforms that had hung in dark parade in bedroom closets in all our houses. I managed to save his officer's cap. She also threw away my Marine uniforms.

If she was sentimental at all, it was a careful, rationed sentiment, mostly limited to the New Hampshire summers of her girlhood, far from her parents. She never told me anything about the day of my birth, for instance.

And my father gave me offhanded play in his journal.

I turned the pages to May 23, 1941, the day of my birth. I was startled to see nothing about me — merely a modestly elegant description of the fine weather and the flowers blooming in our yard. My father took an interest in gardening, passionate about mucking around in the soil but devoid of imagination — rectangular beds, no exotic species, a garden-variety garden.

At last, at the bottom of the entry, I found something along the lines of "Mary gave birth to a son today." He noted the delivery of telegrams of congratulations.

I remembered that he had twice rued journal-keeping to me, scoffing that, "You're always supposed to start with the weather." Obeying this rule, he had started with the weather on the day of my birth. In the newspaper business, this is known as burying the lead.

In fact, he didn't even get the weather right. I looked it up.

As it happened, the day was heavy with omens. The weather started clear and hot, the third day of a hot spell in an ongoing drought. Then it changed. One minute I can imagine chip shots pattering onto greens at Baltusrol Country Club as the sunlight turns oddly thin, the way it can before thunderstorms. On Route 29, a salesman sees the clouds rising in the west and stops to raise the top of his LaSalle convertible.

In the maternity ward at Overlook Hospital in Summit, nurses in stiff white caps may have worried the electricity would go out. And I am born at 4:04 p.m. to Mary Williams Allen, an etherized housewife, and Henry S. Allen Jr. an unprosperous bond broker on the New York Stock Exchange, where the Dow Jones average closes at 116.73, down .08.

I am named Henry Southworth Allen IV but I am called

Rennie until I join the Marine Corps, where "Rennie" lacked viability.

The clouds soon arrive so black that the Yankees-Red Sox game not far away in the Bronx is called in mid-afternoon on account of darkness, a 9-9 tie in the ninth inning. "You couldn't see the ball from the grandstand," James P. Dawson wrote in the New York Times. "By that time everybody had had enough anyhow. It was that kind of game." Lightning set houses on fire, wind blew down trees.

Despite the omens, which I have only just discovered, my birth has an incidental quality to me. It feels like something ending, rather than beginning, as if I'd been drafted from nothingness into life the way men were drafted into the Army. It feels like the luck of the draw, an accident, a slight possibility, nothing more.

My mother liked to tell a story from ten days after I was born. She was home with me and a private nurse. The nurse heard my mother sobbing. She dashed into her bedroom.

"What's the matter?"

"Lou Gehrig died," my mother said. "It was just on the radio."

Gehrig was the great first baseman for the New York

Yankees, the Iron Horse who had died of amyotrophic lateral sclerosis, known afterwards as Lou Gehrig's Disease.

It was hard to know when her sentimentality would make one of its appearances.

As for her own death, 56 years later, at 80, she showed no feelings of grief , gratitude or farewell. Her last words to me, from a gurney in an emergency room: "Just let 'em give me a pill and be done with it."

Leland Street, Chevy Chase.

Chevy Chase

. . . as if he were holding his breath . . .

Now we are three. My mother tugs me across a sunny lawn toward a porch. She has bought a record. She says, "You've got to hear this, Rennie, you're going to love it."

Maybe so, maybe not. When you're three, being noncommittal is a way of life.

My mother mounts the record on the chrome spindle of the turntable. She lowers the tone arm. The record makes a noise I don't like, a thin, adenoidal sound that gives me the same tight, itchy feeling as a taste or smell I don't like. It's like the voice of Arthur Godfrey on the radio — another sound I loathe. Here the sound is Tommy Dorsey's muted trumpets playing "Sunny Side of the Street."

At the end, the Clark Sisters sing their jive lyrics.

"Life's all reet when you dig that beat."

My mother doesn't worry if I like her record. She has a write-it-off hipness, a secular enthusiasm for the offbeat — deli food, convertibles, Stan Kenton's "Intermission Riff," the Clark Sisters singing "Get hip, don't be a drip." She also has a hard cool I rediscovered only recently in some snapshots of her with women friends and, I think, their extravagantly handsome boss from the Office of Price Administration where she worked as a secretary. My father was 8000 miles away, commanding a ship at the months-long battle of Okinawa. She looks startlingly tough in these pictures, posing in sunglasses with a jaunty impatience that suggests she might have a hard time playing the long-waiting Penelope to my father's Odysseus.

This was on Leland Street in Chevy Chase, Maryland, a neighborhood of small lawns and big trees. The house belonged to my grandparents on my mother's side, Paul and Rita Williams, a weighty, three-story place with gables, steep roofs and half-timbering. Inside were shiny floors waxed by a handyman named Sy and enough bedrooms to hold my mother's three younger sisters and a live-in maid, Dorothy, and then my mother, my sister Julie, and me after my father went in the Navy in 1943.

My grandfather — actually my step grandfather — was

Paul Williams, the brilliant and troubled scion of Utah railroad money who moved from New York to Washington in 1933 or 34 under Roosevelt to be special assistant to the attorney general for antitrust. He was a Democrat of a school both aristocratic and Western populist. "Somebody has to look out for the little guy," he told me once.

The somebody-in-chief was Roosevelt.

"Listen to him, he's a great man," my grandmother said one night, stationing me in front of a cathedral-style radio to hear Roosevelt speak. I listened. I didn't understand what he was saying but I remember the noise his voice made, nasal but better than Arthur Godfrey's or the trumpets in "Sunny Side of the Street."

Grandfather Paul Williams at Cornell.

My grandmother, Marguerite, called Rita, was an Irish Catholic from what was once called the village of Flushing in Queens. She'd first married a financial executive named Billy Mitchell, who died of tuberculosis at 29 when my mother was two. While Rita and my toddler mother stayed with her grandmother in Flushing,

Rita went to work as a secretary at the Manhattan law firm where she met Paul Williams.

She had a fussy, intentional way about her. Everything sloped — her shoulders, her eyes, the lines descending from the corners of her mouth. She had a hyper-genteel way of flicking cigarette ashes — she'd lay the cigarette inside the ashtray and roll it until the ash fell off. One of her daughters once said: "She wouldn't go to check the mail without putting on gloves and a hat."

She was the daughter of Julia Ducey, a farm girl from Mt. Airy, Pennsylvania. She would say: "It takes three generations to make a lady." I suppose my mother was the third generation, and indeed, with a mother like Rita and after spending so many years at boarding school she acquired the knack of connecting with other ladies, an upper-class conspiracy, and so Julie and I were invited to the right tea dances, the right black-tie balls where debutantes still danced the Charleston.

Julia's husband, James Darmour, also from Mt. Airy, was a "well-to-do" contracting plumber and head of the Queens anti-Tammany faction of the Democratic Party, according to *The New York Times* in an 1885 story about a death threat from the Black Hand, an Italian extortion operation. He bought a gun and hired two bodyguards to track down the Black Hand extortionists. He lived on to die of Bright's Disease in 1899 at 47. His widow, great-grandmother Julia, started a boarding house that favored gentry such as Fulton Crary who would marry one of the Darmour girls, Frances, and confer on her a genealogy that went back to Robert Fulton and then the Hudson River Dutch.

In my basement I have an ornate embroidered chair that stood at Julia Darmour's dining room table. From it I summon up her house on Amity Street, a Victorian boiled-beef gloom with horsehair sofas, antimacassars, beaded curtains, and steam radiators that knocked in dry air. I could try to find the house and conjure up its ghosts but even if the owners let me in I think I'd find the ghosts had long since been driven out by the glare of the eternal present.

Back to Leland Street: I remember only random incidents.

One day a man next door was watering his lawn with a hose. He asked me if I liked cigar boxes. I said yes. He said he'd give me one. He didn't.

My sister piled up cushions on the porch swing. She climbed up the pile. I told her not to, she could fall. She gave me a none-of-your-business glare I have seen on my mother's face too. I shut up, a failure of courage, I suppose.

She fell over the porch railing and onto the driveway. I felt guilty. After much rushing around by my aunts, they found Julie was not hurt. I was surprised, almost insulted, that I was not blamed.

Fifty years later, my Aunt Cissie said: "You were a sensitive little boy. Maybe too sensitive."

My grandfather, Paul Williams, was descended from 18th century South Carolina cotton planters. They kept moving west. Ten mountain wagons, a carriage, and 30 slaves got them to Kentucky. Later, they moved to Southern Illinois. My great-great-grandfather, Sam Williams, became a Mormon and rode to Salt Lake City in a covered wagon. Shortly afterward he was excommunicated. I can't find out why. His son, Parley Lycurgus Williams, became a lawyer, first as attorney general of the Wyoming territory and then at the center of the railroad business. He was in Promontory Summit, Utah, where the first transcontinental railroad was joined by the driving of the Golden Spike by Leland Stanford. He was said to be in the famous photograph of the locomotives with their cowcatchers touching, but nobody knew which one he was. We had a little velvet bag with a souvenir miniature gold spike in it. We believed it had been cast after the original spike was melted down. This is not true — the original is on display at Stanford University. Other golden spikes were cast but whatever the truth, our little gold spike vanished along with all the family silver along the way.

Grandfather Paul was a burly, athletic man with a square face and thin lips. His daughters (my mother was adopted after her father, Billy Mitchell, died) told me he was a compulsive gambler and a drinker who would rant at the dinner table, concluding with a table-pounding refrain of: "And anybody who doesn't think so is a goddam fool."

When silent, he looked as if he were holding his breath, as if he were unconsciously wrangling with some chronic desperation.

I never heard any nostalgic reveries or funny stories about the Williams household. The daughters all feared but loved him, and regretted that he had not lived up to his brilliance. They complained they couldn't bring friends home for dinner, They'd laugh ruefully about the terrors of riding in a car with him — if a car passed him, he had to pass it back.

His daughters thought his demons came from his fears that he had killed his mother.

Around 1899, when Paul was 12, the family travelled east

in a private railroad car from Salt Lake City to attend his older sister Kate's graduation from Bryn Mawr. The train jolted and he fell against his mother, hitting her breast with his head. Two years later she died of breast cancer. Doctors then believed breast cancer could be caused by a bruise. In old age, living with his daughter, my Aunt Cissie, in Greenwich, Conn., he asked her if she thought he had killed his mother. She told him no, but the damage was long since done.

He got his law degree from Columbia after being sent east to be educated at Exeter, then Cornell, where he was once jailed for assaulting a policeman at a drunken gathering of his secret society. *The New York Times* covered the story.

After graduating from Columbia Law School, he joined the Utah National Guard, and chased Pancho Villa on the Mexican border as a cavalry lieutenant under Pershing. He spent time as a law partner of his father. In World War I he served as a general's aide in France.

His brother Sam, who'd been jailed along with him at Cornell, joined the National Guard too but lost his commission when the Army decided he'd strained his heart rowing at Cornell — "rower's heart," as it was known.

At his own expense he bought an ambulance, outfitted it,

and shipped it to France to serve with the Army. War was required for upper class men, a redeeming adventure for a cohort who had panicked over their loss of manhood — a generation whose portraits show them staring at the camera with indignant frankness, who endured the cold baths and "muscular Christianity" of boarding schools, founded the

THE WASHINGTON TIMES,
TUESDAY, SEPTEMBER 24, 1935

Mr. and Mrs.
In the Future If You Please!

MR. AND MRS. HENRY SOUTHWORTH ALLEN, JR., pictured in their costumes as they left the Cathedral of St. Peter and St. Paul following their marriage there on Saturday in the Bethlehem Chapel. A reception at the Congressional Country Club followed the ceremony. Mr. Allen is the son of Mr. and Mrs. Henry Southworth Allen, Orange, N. J. The bride's parents are Mr. and Mrs. Williams, of Bethesda, Md., and she was formerly Miss Williams. (Harris Ewing Photo).

Newspaper announcement of my parents' wedding.

Boy Scouts, flew and died with the Lafayette Escadrille in France, and tested their manhood against the rapidly closing frontier — Teddy Roosevelt, Owen Wister, Frederic Remington. (As it happened, when Sam got to France the Army returned his commission.)

Manhood: One day Paul told my grandmother he wanted only soup for dinner. He explained that his doctor had said his tonsils had to be taken out. Paul told the doctor to go ahead, take them out. The doctor explained the need for anesthesia and hospitalization. Paul said he didn't need anesthesia. He sat in a chair and the doctor cut out the tonsils.

He had grand Western scope and presumption. When my parents were getting married in 1935, they needed an Episcopal priest.

"Who's the big man?" my grandfather asked.

My parents said that it must be the bishop at National Cathedral. "I'll call him," Paul said. The bishop married my parents in the cathedral's Bethlehem Chapel. The reception was held at Congressional Country Club, where my grandfather also put up the out-of-town guests.

Sam would end up an avocado farmer on land near Santa Monica Boulevard in Los Angeles. He was a drunk and he lived with a Mexican woman, to my grandfather's disgust.

Paul had his own roguery. I gather that he spent money as if spending were an entitlement. He spent it on country clubs, bar bills, and bad bets on horses, bridge, golf, and tennis. The house on Leland Street in Chevy Chase was bought after he came home one night to their earlier, smaller house on Battery Lane in Bethesda and put a bag on the kitchen table in front of my grandmother.

"This is for all the trouble I've caused you," he said, as the daughters told the story.

The bag held $25,000 or more, depending on which daughter was talking. He said he'd won it in the numbers game, an illegal street lottery. This was preposterous — no numbers game ever paid out that much money, worth something like $400,000 in today's dollars. Whatever it was or wherever it came from, my grandmother bought the Leland Street house with it.

When Roosevelt died, my grandfather, scourge of the movie industry, took a job with the Southern California Theatre Owners Association. He bought a big stucco Spanish colonial house on South Bedford Drive in Beverly Hills.

My mother, Aunt Cissie, Cathy, sister Julia, and I drove across the country in a 1941 Ford convertible. In a bid for freedom from Paul, I suspect, we rented a ramshackle beach apartment in Laguna Beach. There was an icebox — I remember the iceman hauling the ice up the rickety outside stairs, a big block melting on the piece of burlap on his shoulder.

Then Julie got sick. We moved back with my grandparents in Beverly Hills. Our nanny was named Mrs. Wright.

She had a sharp face and I disliked her. I made a joke about her, maybe my first joke. I called her "Mrs. Pencil."

My Aunt Nancy, at 15 or so, put lipstick on me. I hated it. I liked Mr. Bray, down the street. He made a wooden rifle for me.

My father came back from the Navy. He was a thin, strong and bald man who had a severe quality in my eyes back then, but not later.

At the door of the garage my mother said: "Ride your tricycle. Show your daddy how you can ride your tricycle."

I didn't want to but I did. He was a stranger. My mother seemed uneasy with him, as if she accepted him not so much as her husband as her fate. In the spring of 1946, driving back to the East Coast I heard Johnny Mercer singing "On the Atchison, Topeka, and the Santa Fe" on the radio. I liked it. Dad told funny stories about the crew on his ship, how the two cooks, Loskutoff and McMaster, used to threaten each other with the baseball bat they used to stir dough. We got stuck behind trucks fouling the air with diesel exhaust, a smell that to me was like a headache, and maybe like Tommy Dorsey's trumpets. Dad

made up a song when we passed 13 brand new Cape Cod
houses, the first of the stupendous post-war building boom.

> Thirteen little white houses,
> standing in a row.
> If you'd like to have one,
> kindly let me know.

Allen house in Fanwood, New Jersey; built in 1946.

Fanwood

Terra Infirma

In 1946, July or August, a year after World War II ended and my father came home from the Pacific to drive us across huge, raw America in our Ford convertible, we moved into a freshly-built three-bedroom house in Fanwood, N.J.

All over America, new houses were erupting from the ground like 17-year locusts — farmland scraped by bulldozers, the staggered racket of carpenters' hammers, the smell of sawdust and glue. They were bought by veterans with mortgages guaranteed by the same G.I. Bill that sent them to college and created a new middle class that made America the greatest country in the history of the world.

After war years lost in drab barracks and berthing compartments, their world was now full of color, pregnant women and the rise of houses like ours, built out of lumber so green that on cold winter nights the freezing sap would creak and snap and I lay in bed reasoning against my fears that a demon was climbing the stairs.

Older people feared the Depression would return. Their houses from before the war had lace tablecloths, cuckoo clocks, antimacassars, radiators, telephones in front halls, and the smell of boiled food. The new houses had the bright, open energy of the future, an energy unimaginable now in the stale, tricky present, which turns out to have been none of the future we took for granted.

Old or new, Fanwood was a town of starter homes for young businessmen like my bond-broker father and homesteads for tradesmen like my friend Billy Odell's father Harold, a printer who commuted along with my father to Manhattan on the Jersey Central railroad, which still ran steam locomotives. You'd hear them on icy mornings, the wheels trying to grip the rails, WHUFF WHUFF Whuffuffuffuff . . . and begin again. Billy and I would try to drop snowballs into their smokestacks from the Sheelen's Avenue bridge. We had been warned that if we succeeded, the locomotive would blow up. We kept trying.

There was a sense of buoyancy, of ascent into October blue skies — smoke from raked leaves and the cheers that billowed up from the Scotch Plains High School football bleachers I sneaked under to admire the colliding of high school boys and the mystery of the cheerleaders in their short skirts. So much was possible and everything was real.

Of course real also meant Russian atom bombs and polio, harelips, club feet, crossed eyes, and hunchbacks that could not be fixed then. There were shortages too, right after the war — cars, tires, and refrigerators, which people still called iceboxes. We got lucky and found a used one for sale at Snuffy's Restaurant in Scotch Plains, the neighboring town. The only sneakers at Inglesby's store were ugly brown high-tops.

My Uncle Peter gave me his hero's medal from putting out the fire in his B-24 over Europe. My father made me give it back. One night at our dinner table Peter got drunk and cried, telling us about a saboteur who'd been planting bombs on landing gear. When the wheels came up after take-off the planes blew up. The saboteur got caught. The commanding officer said: "Take him out back and shoot him." Peter couldn't stop crying.

Dad was sinewy and thin. He'd gone through Okinawa, three months of kamikazes, and his face still held his skipper's toughness. He kept his uniforms in his closet for decades. Saturday mornings in Fanwood he wore a checked lumberjack shirt, red-and-black, when he cut down trees to make a front lawn. I liked to watch. How slowly they moved through the sky when they started to fall.

Pulling the stumps was the hardest part. He argued with Bill Miller from down the street about the best way to do it.

"You'll never get it out that way," Mr. Miller said. "You have to cut the tap root."

"You don't pull these stumps that way, Bill."

"It's the only way you'll get that one out."

"Not this one," my father said, setting the trap. "I'm not sure this one is going to come out at all."

Bill offered to bet $5 that he could do it.

It was nearly dawn when Bill, working by lantern light, got the stump out. My father paid the $5 and bragged about it for the rest of his life.

Technology would not so much save the world as promise to take it where it was destined to go. *Popular Mechanics* said that soon we'd ride on monorails and commute by "auto-gyros." For a moment, tiny 26-horsepower Crosley cars were the future, along with "pre-fab" houses and the Flying Wing, an airplane of spooky beauty without a fuselage, just wings and a tendency to crash. We waited for televisions — there was a shortage. We drove to Plainfield one night and bought tickets to see Hitler's huge Mercedes touring car.

Every week, magazines told us who we were. We discovered not only that Jackson Pollock existed but that he was an artistic giant when *Life* magazine asked if he was "the greatest living painter in the United States."

"It's not painting," my father said. He was artistic. He painted landscapes. He wrote funny songs and directed the musical numbers for the annual show of the Philathelians, the Fanwood theater troupe. I remember him at our upright piano, rehearsing an Andrews Sisters number with three girls who wore jeans with the cuffs turned way up and their fathers' white shirts hanging out.

It was the new look. Gone were the cardigans and saddle shoes my aunts had worn during the war. Teenage boys stopped slicking their hair back and instead used Brylcreem and a lot of brushing to make their hair rise up from their foreheads in a "wave."

I climbed trees, I took piano lessons, I was a skinny kid with braces and a little-boy head shaped like a lightbulb. I went for hikes in the Watchung Mountains above Seeley's Pond. I slept in the bedroom over the garage — no attic so the rain on the roof was loud, the best sound in the world, racking me with waves of goosebumps and happy shuddering.

My boyhood happened with the usual triumphs and despairs, tendencies toward self-loathing and talky excitability, hours reading on my bed, building tree houses, softening my Bobby Avila second-baseman's glove with neatsfoot oil, lying on the dining room floor to watch a black-and-white television — *Howdy Doody* and *Ed Sullivan*. At School 4, I saw no point in doing the group assignments — a traffic safety mural, singing songs from many lands — instead resigning myself to the loneliness of being what I assumed to be the smartest kid in the class, watching the clock and reading books of fairy tales hidden on my lap.

In fifth grade at School 1 in Scotch Plains, I defied the scorn I'd suffered for my flailing athletic incompetence and signed up for an after-school softball league. Sides were chosen. I was chosen second to last, the last being a boy with cerebral palsy.

In the last inning of a playoff game, we were losing with two out and players on base, our last chance. It was my turn to bat. This could not be allowed to happen. My teammates formed a screen around me, saying, "Where's Allen? Did he go home?"

Then a redeeming angel appeared and conferred on me the heart of a hero.

"It's my ups," I said, in a tone that was adamant and new even to me. My teammates swore and stamped the ground with frustration.

Right now, as an old man writing in a winter studio, I can still see the third pitch arcing toward me and feel my angel-driven bat hit the ball with a fat softball crack, drive it over the infield, the outfield and then into the trees beyond the outfield, seeming to accelerate as it flew, going, going, gone. I circled the bases and was buried in a pile of new best friends.

That home run changed my life. Through the years, despite dangerous despairs, errors and the horrors of love gone wrong, there was always a place in me where a softball was climbing forever through a May afternoon, and I knew I could step up to the plate and do what had to be done. I still wonder what happened to the real hero of this story, that boy with cerebral palsy,

We would live in our Fanwood house for eight years.

I must have wondered aloud about what it would be like to go back someday.

My father said, "Never go back. Everything is smaller."

This made sense. Short children remember tall houses. The more important things are in our memories, the larger they seem. Nevertheless at the moment my father said it, I vowed to remember the correct size of our Fanwood house, my grandfather's house in Orange, my Uncle Fulton's house in New Hampshire, all our houses and our neighbors' houses, forever. I also vowed to go back.

In 2004, 50 years later, I went back, driving down Route 22 and taking a left into Scotch Plains. The school where I hit the home run had burned, sadly — it was a beautiful, turreted Victorian building designed by Stanford White — and the baseball field was gone. Next to it, though, my barbershop was still there — I remember the Italian guys laughing at me when I asked if you had to go to college to be a barber.

"College!" they said. How they laughed.

A secret loner all my life, I asked questions to stay in touch with the world.

I turned my car toward my old neighborhood. I found that I had remembered the houses to exact scale, as I had vowed to do, but dear God, what had happened to the yards, slopes, the whole landscape? The shape of the land seemed to have lurched like a dreaming animal. I felt as if I were losing my balance. It had nothing to do with importance or my changed height. It had everything to do with the fact that I'd been wrong about memory — it is not the rock of reality but clay. Most unsettling was the part of Russell Road we called Slocum's Hill when we hurtled down its vertiginous slope on our Flexible Flyers, whole daredevil snow days of belly-flopping toward a bonfire at the bottom of the hill. Now, time had worn Slocum's Hill to a rise so gentle you could ascend it in a wheelchair.

I had been wrong for half a century, the lesson being that memory is not some ark of a covenant made in childhood but only another variable, random as clouds. Proust said that we don't remember the past, we create it. Faulkner said the past is never dead, it isn't even past. They are both right. Memory is so complicated that it takes a contradiction to define it.

I parked a block down Russell Road across from the Yokels' old house, a little brick Tudor where I learned to play Old Maid and Blind Man's Bluff and Mrs. Yokel, known for being "high-strung," had a white stitch scar across her throat from thyroid surgery.

I wanted to approach my house on foot, as if I were a kid again, as if I could catch it or myself unawares.

I turned down Paterson Road. Gravel driveways were paved now. Azaleas were blooming in ice cream colors where

I remembered the formality of rhododendrons. A half-century of lawn fertilizer, paint, and money had made everything look disquietingly perfect, like scale models in museums. These houses once had watched over me like aunts and uncles. Now they had taken on the implacable opacity of blind people who didn't know who I was and smiled only to be polite. I felt transparent, like a ghost.

On a far corner I could see the Bergdorf's brown-shingled house. Doug ran a miniature golf course on Route 22. They were Christian Scientists and long ago the women of the neighborhood cringed to hear Ann's cries through open windows as she gave birth at home on a warm day, attended only by a reader reciting the Bible aloud, or the works of Mary Baker Eddy. In the colonial on a near corner, Adele Parkhurst, who had once sung on the radio, seduced our cat Bocko with chopped liver and cream.

My house, 91 Willoughby Road, slid slowly into view like a spaceship in a movie. The garage emerged from behind the Van Blaricom house, the driveway bearing a Honda Accord. Then the front steps on the corner of the four-window front, and the slight second-story overhang, a hint of New England painted warm gray now with maroon shutters instead of the universal chalk white with black shutters of 50 years ago. A split-rail fence — could it possibly be the same one my father had put up? The trees were bigger, I expected that, and the lawn was perfect. My father once gave me a kitchen knife and set me to cutting out dandelions for 15 cents a bushel — I saw that the fastest way to a

My sister Julia and me, Easter, 1946.

bushel was to take huge divots in the lawn, which ended up cratered like an 81mm mortar test range. Now it was perfection, a fairway, but didn't it used to slope sharply when it got near the street? Apparently not — it ran level to the pavement (no longer tar that turned soft on hot days). More terra infirma. What a pointless trick for my memory to play on me.

I stared at the house. Here is, there was, there had been.

I wouldn't be able to go inside. A month before I had called the couple who lived there, told them I was a journalist at *The Washington Post* and I had once lived in their house. I wanted to write a piece about returning home after 50 years, the phantasmagoria of memory. I wondered if I might have permission to look inside.

The woman on the other end panicked.

"What do you want?" she kept asking across what seemed like a huge and growing distance. "What do you want?" And finally: "This is impossible. No. This is impossible."

She was afraid. Of what?

A man was mowing the lawn of the old Van Blaricom house. I explained why I was taking pictures of the house across Willoughby Road. He was a retired baseball scout named Bob Buob, age 72. I asked him about the frightened response I'd gotten from the woman on the phone. With some care, he said: "They don't mix much, they keep to themselves."

I pointed to the far back corner of his yard where once I had stepped in a nest of miner's bees that stung me dozens of times as I sprinted home.

He said: "I dynamited that nest years ago. They haven't been back."

A link between us felt good, even if the link was hornets.

I asked if people still left their doors unlocked.

He said: "No more. That age is gone."

Down Willoughby Road, Jack Lubin, a contractor working on his truck, said: "It's not safe. We live in the middle of a bubble. All around us, you've got your element that drives through here, it's not safe. The kids are all in organized sports, or they're inside their houses on computers."

Have there been burglaries on Willoughby Road?

"Nah," he said.

So what are they scared of? He shrugged as if to say: if you don't know I can't explain.

America had changed. Crime, drugs, fear instilled by governments seeking power by scaring us with Communism, then child molesters and terrorists. The klaxon of the media never stops. A failure to fear is a civic irresponsibility. The signs on highways and subways say: "See something? Say something."

Where were the girls jumping rope or playing hopscotch? No kids on bikes. I'd be an outsider now on the blue Schwinn that gave me my first taste of freedom. I saw a few women out on lawns with toddlers. Young couples, starter-home types, walked pit bulls — I saw three of them on one block.

I tried introducing myself as I'd introduced myself to

10,000 people in my life as a journalist. They kept their distance from me. Perhaps I was a ghost to them, as if I'd risen from an Indian burial ground. Or they were afraid. Or they thought I was masquerading as a journalist, some sort of scam — possibly my proprietary instinct toward Willoughby Road showed through, giving me the air of a con man. Or maybe it was just New Jersey. What's it to you? Who wants to know?

I was a stranger in a familiar land, with the odd quality, perhaps, of seeming entitled and bewildered at the same time.

There was the next-door Burgards' stone-fronted bungalow where Andrea hid under the piano during thunderstorms? Her father had a New Jersey accent — glottal stops removed the Ts from "bottle," and "toilet" sounded like "terlet." He worked in a factory, and at night he was a soda jerk.

Was that Barbie Wolf's shabby ranch house where her father answered the door in his underpants and the biggest and most beautiful apple tree in the world blossomed in the backyard, a mystical explosion one spring morning in my little-boy mind?

Whatever happened to sandboxes? Are they too simple and cheap to interest children nowadays?

Was that the white frame house where Mrs. Totten gave me piano lessons while her stroke-stricken stockbroker husband moaned in a bedroom upstairs? Only by deduction could I conclude that a stucco house was Dr. Farenchek's, the same chain-link fence and forsythia bushes whose frail radiance was once a sign to me that spring was finally here for sure, other heralds being milk that tasted of early onion grass (this being back when milk came from cows that grazed in local pastures) and the skunk cabbage that really smelled like skunks in the swampy woods.

Those woods were gone, along with their mysteries, filled now with houses that look flimsy in their ordinariness.

After I passed the Williams' old house, where their son Tommy used to listen to St. Louis Browns games on the car radio, I could see into my old backyard.

Still there, unchanged, covered with fresh white gravel, was the patio my father dug into the lawn so he and my mother could sit on chaises lounges, read magazines, and drink gin and tonics in the shade, a touch of homemade elegance for people whose birthright to it had gotten tangled up in a sort of socioeconomic probate, back in the Depression and during the war.

I remember my father out there, quoting Hamlet to me, apropos of nothing but the music of the words:

'Tis now the very witching time of night,
When churchyards yawn and hell itself breathes out
Contagion to this world.

Was it two ounces of gin — or more — that brought on my parents' happiness? One of the few unconditional gifts that parents can bestow on the children is moments of their own happiness, gin or no.

My mother's sisters, Cathy and Cissie, worked for NBC in Manhattan. They brought their boyfriends out to sit on the patio. In the living room, next to the fireplace, were armchairs where my parents read the evening newspapers my father brought home from New York. In the summer my mother spread rush rugs. On Saturday nights there were parties around the piano. My sister and I would peer from the stairs, studying grown-up fun. Next to the couch was a little wooden secretary where I watched my father write a letter to Sen. Robert Taft, and I once drew pictures of Abraham Lincoln from a penny.

On one of the bookshelves, the dark collected works of

Conrad were testimony to my father's youthful romance with the sea.

The house was like a spore of my grandfather's house in Orange, the attic holding the DNA of lost worlds — spats and a collapsible top hat my father had worn with   his white tie and tails, wooden-shafted golf clubs, an elongated Mercer Beasley tennis racket in a wing-nut press, a bugle, a ukulele, a bamboo fly rod resting on the beams, a steamer trunk my father opened to find a plaid blanket.

"This was Jack Huntington's blanket," he said, referring to a Princeton classmate who owned the Friendship sloop on which my father tried to cross the Atlantic.

"What happened to Jack Huntington?" I asked.

"He killed himself," my father said.

"Why?"

"I don't know. He was unhappy, I guess."

I used to rummage through Dad's bureau drawers — sheath knives, a money clip, watch chains, a belt buckle, the paraphernalia of manhood. And his closet, with shined shoes lined up dark and precise, his Navy uniforms, his regimental stripe neckties.

Throughout the house, sterling silver porringers were

ashtrays. Wedding presents from 1935 provided bed linens, blankets (which I still have) and tableware that was magnum grade sterling silver, so clumsy in my boyish hand that every dinner ended with a halo of rice or peas around my chair. Tired of polishing silver, my mother wanted stainless steel but we couldn't afford it.

Once, my father bought her a salad bowl in New York, formal with a silver base and shiny black wood that couldn't be washed, but only rubbed clean with oil, lest it crack and dull. In a fever of pleasing, he forgot and washed it with soap and water after dinner. The finish was ruined.

My mother was frantic with frustration. "You ruin every-thing," she said.

This gentleman, this brave ship captain, this feller of tall trees, my father, stood stymied in the kitchen door. He would keep on believing he could make my mother happy with pres-ents, a bottle of Chanel No. 5 every Christmas, porcelain mice for her collection, charms for her charm bracelet. The first Christmas after he died I bought her a bottle of Chanel No. 5. She showed me her collection of the bottles he had given her, most of them full. But she had kept them.

He drove her mad with his sentimentality and illusions.

She may have worried him with her drinking, if not then, a few years later. At 18 she had married him for love and to escape her family. At 18 you take money for granted but as it happened there would never be much of it. He lacked the opportunism, the predatory instinct that Wall Street rewards. He stayed there because my grandfather had insisted on it, maybe assuming that money would come as if by the grace of God. In the meantime, we had a used Ford sedan with no heater. For summer vacations we visited relatives. My grandfather paid for my braces.

At 37 my father still had no idea what he wanted to do beyond his lost dreams of seafaring or writing musical comedies. He took aptitude tests at Stevens Institute in Hoboken. The tests said he'd make a good salesman. He broke with his father and left Wall Street. Through connections at Wallace Silversmiths in Wallingford, Conn., he got a beginner's job travelling the country selling tableware to hotels.

Wallace gave him America's best territory — New York, with its million jewelry stores. The Jewish jewelers found him exotic, with his Princeton WASP demeanor, and he found them fascinating. He would come home glowing with delight at a new Yiddish word he'd learned.

He made more money now. At a cottage we rented on

the Jersey shore, he got a telegram awarding him a $1500 bonus — worth nearly ten times as much now. He kept staring at it with wordless gratitude and wonderment.

We bought a dishwasher, nicknamed Fifi. We bought a new red Ford convertible with Continental kit — a tire on the back. A bonanza of middling size came when my grandfather died and left us $50,000. That's when we left our starter home in Fanwood for a neighborhood in Westfield called Wychwood, where the boys I met were proud to inform me that no Jews could buy houses there. I hated it, but then I'd gotten to hate Fanwood too, prey to the belief that my unhappiness would vanish if we lived somewhere else. In fact, my furious melancholy sprang not from Fanwood or Freudian trauma but merely an inborn trait that would come and go until the medications of my middle age.

We lived in Westfield for a year until my father was offered the job of assistant sales manager in Wallingford. We bought a soulless white hilltop house with a winding staircase on nearly three-quarters of an acre that I hated mowing. Its terrace overlooked the town, including a fireworks factory that blew up one day while I was burning trash in the back yard, sending a tidy mushroom cloud into the sky. The house had been owned by a family named Downey, whose son,

John, was a CIA agent who'd been shot down over Communist China in 1952.

"It gives me the willies," my mother would say. "He's in prison over there, thinking about this house."

My parents became part of a hard-drinking crowd of factory town aristocrats, some of them friends from before the war. The wives spent afternoons visiting each other, bringing their dogs along, and lying on chaises to work on their tans. There were parties. Everybody stood around my father's piano and sang the old college songs. As the night wore on and the parties acquired alcohol's two-dimensional hilarity, the crowd would line up for a parade, called a "pea-rade." To a record of "The Yellow Rose of Texas" they marched around the living room behind a Texan wife who bore a fire poker for a baton.

Here was everything my parents seemed to want, but things were falling apart. My mother would drink so much she fell into trances at the dinner table, and my father ignored her — not a word was to be said.

I knew something was very wrong one Christmas eve when Julie and I discovered our parents had failed to buy a Christmas tree. They said it was too much trouble. Abandoning family rituals is a sign of some dark encroachment on life as we have known it. Around then, my father's Auntie Marge offered to give us a family camp on Snow's Pond near the base of Cape Cod, but that was too much trouble too.

We would own one more house — in Pennsylvania when the Hamilton Watch Company bought Wallace and hired my father as sales manager for sterling silver. It was a beautiful old stone house on a millstream in Lancaster County. But my parents failed to find a crowd to party with. Debts swelled to pay tuitions. My father got fired. I quit college to enlist in the Marine Corps. My sister quit college to work as a secretary in New York. My parents went back to Connecticut and a string of rentals and declining jobs.

The last hurrah was Julie's wedding in the late '60s. Family and old friends convened for a night wedding at St. Paul's Episcopal Church in Wallingford. I was an usher. I wore my father's white tie and tails, the ones I had admired in the attic in Fanwood. I was the last Allen man to wear them. They fit perfectly. They would be auctioned off, like most of my parents' possessions.

Decades after that, after walking Fanwood's streets on a May afternoon, I came back to Willoughby Road and saw the Honda Accord had left the driveway. No one was home.

I walked to the front door and stared through the windows into the living room. It was the same, with shinier floors. I was unmoved. I saw it would all be the same, with shinier floors and different-colored paint. Fine. No nostalgia, no epiphany. No need to visit after all.

Standing on the front steps I wrote the ungracious owners a gracious note that was not entirely without malice. I praised them for the wonderful care they'd taken care of the house and the property.

A month before, in that strange telephone call, the panicky woman of the house had kept asking me what I wanted. Now, I knew that I wanted nothing. I put the note in the mailbox and wondered if, like a ghost, it would cost them any sleep.

The whiskey of choice, aka "hooch."

A Note on Drinking

The floor bears you up in quiet triumph.

Drinking keeps popping up in this chronicle. Nothing unusual here. WASPs are frequently the butts of booze jokes (Whiskypalians) and prompters of phrases such as "functional alcoholism as a way of life."

So it can be — a ritual, a redemption, a raison d'être, and the source of what people with meaningless lives desire as much as anything — something to do tomorrow. As sure as the earth turns, cocktail hour will come round again.

The first drink of the day! You hear the ice hiss, smell the fallen-apple sweetness of it. You may wait for a moment in an homage to abstinence, then hoist it like a cornerstone, and in a moment or two your house feels like a haven, as if someone had just lighted a fire. The floor bears you up in quiet triumph. There's a sense of accidental pause, as at the top of a Ferris wheel when you look out and the world is full of amazing possibility. How paramount! Your sense of self and soul seems to enlarge. You feel nostalgia, not for the past but for the present, right now, along with whatever future is in the near offing.

I wrote similar words on the hundredth anniversary of F. Scott Fitzgerald's birth. He is said to have said: "First you take a drink. Then the drink takes a drink. Then the drink takes you."

It's not just WASPs — alcoholism is an equal-opportunity employer. More than 10 percent of American children have an alcoholic parent, according to the National Institutes of Health. They're apt to grow up with a sense of reality as an arbitrary, provisional or dangerously unpredictable thing. They may grow up like Fitzgerald's Gatsby, experiencing "the unreality of reality, a promise that the rock of the world was founded securely on a fairy's wing."

This is a lovely belief if you have the money, class, or whiskey to support it.

WASPworld a half-century ago was full of people whose family money was running out but they still had the class and the whiskey. They could spot other people like them — they'd see a couple across a beach on Martha's Vineyard and say, "They look nice," meaning they could be asked over for cocktails. People were either "nice" or they were gently dismissed, as in, "They're the ones with that big Cadillac, aren't they?"

They had friends in common at yacht clubs or college or boarding school. They believed in getting good grades but not too good, lest one be branded a "grind." They went to football games and never, ever booed. They rarely said "rich," using slang terms instead: "well-off" or "loaded" or "rolling in it." They were modest, these people of 50 years ago, cultivating a genteel shabbiness. They drove Ford station wagons and drank cheap whiskey they called "hooch," a slang term from Prohibition. They drank a lot of it.

While reading about families with alcoholic parents, I read that about five percent of American adults are "heavy drinkers." This was defined as having two or more drinks a day, a drink being 1.5 ounces of 80-proof spirits.

What? I was astonished. This is "heavy drinking"? Three ounces a day? I noticed that a snobbery informed my astonishment, as if three ounces a day might be heavy drinking for other people, but my family, with its breeding, could hold its liquor. A normal intake was as much as eight ounces of whiskey a day — four two-ounce drinks a day in a daily ritual of two cocktails before dinner, a highball afterward and then a nightcap, all measured carefully from a shot glass.

"Pouring from the bottle makes drunks," my father told me once as he prepared another round of drinks for the family gathered under the maple tree behind Uncle Fulton's house in New Hampshire. He did not mention that pouring from a shot glass makes drunks too. Nor did he understand why he believed in these rules, and there were lots of them.

No drinking in the morning, although on weekends one could drink when "the sun was over the yardarm." I once saw my parents split a fifth of whiskey before lunch. I remember their glow of conspiratorial satisfaction, basking in the breezes of another planet far, far away.

No drinking by yourself, which really meant no getting caught drinking by yourself, pulling from the bottle in the pantry, in the desk drawer.

You had to be able to drink a lot and show no effects. This was particularly admired in women. Drinking and holding it was equated with manliness and New Englanders admired women who had a little manliness.

"She's got a hollow leg," people would say. "She can drink any man under the table."

Once, telling me about America back when it was a real

country with real men, my father said: "The standard shot at the bar in the Waldorf-Astoria hotel used to be four ounces."

Abstinence was grounds for exile. A teetotaler was not welcome at cocktail hour. Drinking was not just an entitlement, it was an obligation.

Old axiom: Never trust a man who doesn't drink.

On the other hand, one did not ask for a third drink, one rattled the ice in an empty glass.

The host's response: "Freshen that up for you?"

If the liquor was not held well, squalor was to be ignored. I have seen a grandmother fall downstairs while a Christmas party raged on around her, paying no heed. I have heard the best-bred people shriek obscenities at each other. "You didn't even comb your fucking hair!" I recall a drunken hostess shouting at her husband: "I'm so ugly! I'm so ugly!"

The next morning there would be guilty hangovers, but the earth was always turning toward redemption in the form of the next first drink of the day.

The rules would seem to have existed to protect you from alcoholism or at least preserve civilized behavior, but their existence was much more pernicious. They existed to disprove your worries that you had a drinking problem. As

AA members will say, if you're worried that you have a drinking problem you have a drinking problem. But wait! You obey all the rules, you don't drink in the morning, you hold your liquor, you don't drink by yourself, therefore you do not have a drinking problem. A dollop? Freshen that up for you?

Drinking — heavy drinking, problem drinking — puts you in spiritual debt. It is a loan that will be paid back with interest that compounds with every drink in the form of a hangover, a drunk-driving bust, the disintegration of a business, a nervous system or a family as the debt accrues.

It comes to have a life of its own. Soon it nags you, then demands its rights and finally it threatens you like an alien beast, becoming what the Irish call "the creature." It's as if you were a knight in tarnished armor, and alcohol were both the steed you rode to combat and the dragon you fought.

From bright to dark: from blithe ownership of reality and a polite glow that civilizes the dinner hour to the squalor of lies, grandiosity, panic, amnesia, paranoia, bullying, insomnia, bankruptcy, organ failure, self-pity, and the exuding of bodily foulness by a pole-axed nervous system.

After he got sober, John Cheever wrote: "In the earliest religious myths and legends, alcohol is one of the first gifts of the Gods. . . . The belief that to be drunk is to be blessed is very deep. . . . To die of drink is sometimes thought a graceful and natural death — overlooking wet brains, convulsions, delirium tremens, hallucinations, hideous automobile accidents, and botched suicides. . . . To drink oneself to death was not in any way alarming, I thought, until I found that I was drinking myself to death."

Life begins again with the first drink of the day, be it an evening martini of geometric perfection, or a frantic two-handed morning struggle to drink yourself into the steadiness required for shaving.

Drinking plagued my family for several generations, maybe more. It was like a place we lived. I became addicted to alcohol too, but I recovered. I remember with a poignant yearning what it meant, or seemed to mean — an enlargement of the soul, an afflatus, the sense of infinite possibility. When I went through the horror of quitting, I discovered drinking means not just nothing but less than nothing — it repays your love by sucking out your soul.

Storm clouds at a Chebeague Island house (drawing by the author).

Summer Houses

. . . where you become the real you . . .

There are all the summer houses in America — a Jersey Shore Victorian with porches where wicker creaks and ice cubes chime, a board-and-batten camp in Minnesota with a wall-mounted muskellunge that frightens the grandchildren, a Maine cottage with bare-stud walls and a cold, sharp smell from the fireplace, a Colorado cabin whose trophy antlers bristle in the firelight.

Even though you spend as little as two weeks a year in them, they're where you become the Real You, where the universe seems to acknowledge your existence with oddly personal weather — thrilling thunderstorms, clouds that at any moment will "burn off" to resurrect the bright glory of surf and its musical boom. Constellations puncture the firmament on country-black nights. Up at the lake. Down at the shore.

My family had them too, both random rentals and family houses. In New Hampshire, Sheep Rock smelled of Uncle Fulton's Bond Street pipe tobacco and the sweet resin of the Pine Room where the children slept on army bunks. My mother had spent her girlhood summers with Fult and Aunt Fan and she seemed happier there than anywhere else, which might have made me happier there than anywhere else.

I remember her sitting in an Adirondack chair under a maple tree at cocktail hour while hired hands drove cows past the house after milking. Day was done. If anyone commented on the good weather, she'd wave her cigarette away from her mouth and say: "It is a beauteous evening, calm and free. The holy time is quiet as a nun, breathless with adoration." That was Wordsworth, whom she seemed to regard as a bit of a wet smack. I wrote my own poem, too.

THE COCKTAIL HOUR

Under the spreading maple tree,
cocktails at last. A buoyancy
in peeling Adirondack chairs
redeems old failings, shopworn cares.

A splash? A dividend? One more?
A dollop for you, Commodore?

Life's dinginess dissolves like fog.
Aunt Ag slips Triscuits to the dog.

Clearness returns, as in a pool
where color trembles, deep and cool,
beneath Narcissus' earnest face.
This is the time, this is the place

that mended lives once more are whole,
despairs replaced with newfound soul
while down the road the Chickerings' cows
go back to pasture. Here, we browse

through ancient stories once more true,
the same old laughter once more new.
Sweet hooch averts life's eyeless stare,
as twilight soothes the day's long glare.

The cigarettes begin to glow
as shadows of the twilight grow.
Things seem to have a point again.
Somebody says: "Remember when. . . ."

The children watch the grown-ups drink.
They sense a happiness and think
it will be theirs too when they're grown —
not knowing that it's drink alone.

On my father's side of the family there was Snow's Pond amid the cranberry bogs and piney woods near Cape Cod. From the porch, seen through the trees, the pond had the quality of something levitating. My mother's sister Cissie owned an old house on Chebeague Island, in Casco Bay, Maine. She had five children. We found our own rental house with a water view through the birch trees, and a lobsterman for a neighbor.

These houses were centers of extended cousinhood, family seats we shared with aunts, uncles, cousins, grandparents, in-laws. Snapshots accumulated, stories were told over and over. But this is true of so many summer houses. Essentially, they were no different than anyone else's.

Let us generalize, then, and say, as an example, that you pull up to whatever summer house it might be after driving all day Saturday in the heat.

You look around. None of the neighbors are back from swimming yet and the front-walk petunias look neglected in the glare — there's a festive but deserted quality to things. You open the door. The house is hot. The cleaning woman, who lives in the village, closed all the windows that morning in case there was a thunderstorm.

"Open some windows!" everybody says.

The heat is full of the smell of blankets, sand, mildew, a freshly swept fireplace, and damp couch cushions. There is a buckled map hanging on the wall. There is a pile of the last tenant's newspapers next to the fireplace. There is a sense of possibilities. You turn on a light, and turn it off again. You turn on the cold water, which runs hot. Then you carry your suitcase upstairs.

Your bedroom is very hot.

You open the suitcase. You packed it only last night, but it looks like an ungainly time capsule from another life. You wonder why you brought those dress shoes. You sense that once again, you won't finish that copy of *Anna Karenina*. You don't care. You like not caring because it means you are starting to be On Vacation. All happy summer houses are alike — you never wear your dress shoes or finish *Anna Karenina* in any of them.

You pull out a bureau drawer. You smell the parched wood and the old shelf paper thumbtacked to it, a smell that is ancient and utterly personal, like the smell of the double-ended wooden spoons you once used to eat ice cream from Dixie Cups.

This smell lasts till you open the window.

The wind fills the room instantly, like a cool noise. You

look at the excellent sky over the treetops. You hear a flag rolling and snapping, with the hollowness that sound has near water. You breathe deeply. You take off your clothes. You put on your bathing suit. You have every intention of going swimming before dinner. Just for a moment, though, you lie down on the unmade bed. You close your eyes. You make a mental note to water those petunias. You are in your summer house. You are asleep.

Back in the unreal city, everything is rules. At a summer house, everything feels like tradition instead: drinks you will never drink anywhere else (brandy shrubs, Pimm's Cups), Mom always going first in the outdoor shower so she gets the sun-warmed water, playing Parcheesi on rainy days, using jelly jars for drinking glasses.

Everything is permitted (as long as you hang up your bathing suit and don't track sand in the house) and everything is real. Your parents won't let you take a bus at home, but here you can take the boat all the way across the lake to town where you ask for a weather prediction from a cashier.

"Off and on," she says.

You feel like a kid in a Disney movie, orphaned and entitled at the same time, wanting nothing more than the blond hair and the impossible tans of the summer carpenters, who have great trucks and beach parties (which, as it turns out, are not quite as great as you'd thought they'd be).

Summer houses are tiny cottages on motorboat lakes, jostling with all the other cottages in a kind of laundry-flapping, lotion-sticky, barbecue proximity that verges on the sexual. They are mammoth old brown-shingled dowagers groaning in the wind off the ocean. They are Adirondack camps with rusting screens that stick out like beer bellies, and Michigan fishing camps that have no locks on the doors. They are the gloomy dinosaurs of Mantoloking, N.J., asleep amid the hydrangeas.

They are cabins, camps, lodges, farmhouses, A-frames, ex-barns, not so much built as moored on the edge of dunes, lakes, valleys, cliffs, harbors, and national parks. They are more Northern than Southern, more Eastern than Western, not so much architecture as an opportunity for metaphysical multiplication of porches, decks, and outdoor staircases. They are cottages with locks that are stiff from the salt air, and very old cars cooking inside closed garages. They are group houses where you bridge the psychic gap between fraternity parties and the vacations you will someday take your children on. They are rental houses with the mysterious owner's closet, which is locked until you find the key and open it one rainy afternoon to find only some canned tomatoes, a butter-fly collection and a bottle of Old Mr. Boston sloe gin.

They have pasts, instant history: the crayoned j'accuse you find under a porch cushion — "Susan is a liar" — or the old man at the boatyard showing you a walrus skull he pulled up in a fishing net. Who was Susan, when was the walrus?

There are the Indians, animals, and primeval cataclysms that left their names on these places: Chincoteague, Seal Cove, Mackinaw Island, Crater Lake, Thunder Mountain. You return to a tribal comity. Instead of asking for my binoculars, you ask for the binoculars. Not my air mattress but the air mattress. Everyone's. The tribe's. You all pick blueberries. You all shoot the .22.

"Your mother is the shot in this family," you tell the kids, putting the tin cans on the fence posts.

"It's not true," she says. "You say that every year."

"It's true!" the children shout.

With an air of bewildered and dutiful modesty she knocks down each can with one shot, even the little cat food can. Everyone cheers.

"You're all such fools about this," she says. "Every year."

They are houses on islands in Maine where a north wind

brings down light so intense it seems on the verge of fragmenting into chunks the size of ping-pong balls, a light that also creates shadows with a pleasantly alarming coolness. In September, these houses are shut for the winter, sometimes in a ritual known as an "Augusta closing," in which you turn the mirrors to the walls, put a stone in the toilet, put newspaper up the chimney and cover the lampshades, although nobody is quite sure why anymore, anymore than they know why it's called an "Augusta closing."

They are where: You would find a faded 48-star flag in a drawer and raise it every morning. You eat corn on the cob and taste the mosquito repellent on your hands. You fall in love on purpose. You save your dog from drowning. You sit out on the porch on a starry night, the whole family singing "The Battle Hymn of the Republic."

They are houses you rent one after another, a new one every summer until all the rusty hibachis, thundering shower stalls and landlady-needlepoint samplers become the same.

They are houses you go back to year after year.

"It never changes," your father says as you drive through town, past the five-and-dime with its beach chairs and umbrellas out front, past the Dairy Queen where you always buy a cone for the dog too.

"They painted the windmill at the miniature golf course," your mother says.

"Well, dammit, it needed painting," says your father, who is irritable in the manner of sentimental men.

"But they didn't even have a windmill last year," your brother says, thus beginning a debate about which miniature golf course you're talking about, and is miniature golf the same as Putt-Putt, and if so what is pitch 'n' putt? This debate will become a sly running joke through the whole stay at the house, where, fortunately, nothing has changed (as your father notes in a voice that invites no contradiction) except for some new planks in the porch.

They are where you fall deepest into the ur-illusion of America, which is that you can endlessly invent and reinvent yourself. You bring along your old brushes and paints from college, and the denim skirt you used to paint in, and suddenly the colors don't turn to mud and the trees and houses don't look like they're floating. Is it possible that you're really an artist after all?

"Remember those pictures we saw at the art gallery?" you ask. "Isn't this every bit as good as they are? Really. I want to know. Tell me why it isn't."

"Beats me," he says.

They are a sort of duty-free zone for drinkers, a place where the back-brain demon-philosopher of alcoholism lets them have all they want.

"Sun's over the yardarm," they say at noon. Or they tear open the beers as soon as the tennis game ends. Or they wait all day for cocktail hour.

After a while there arises the tocsin of ice rattling in empty glasses.

"Freshen that up for you?"

The children watch their parents drink. They don't understand the chemical smugness their parents feel, and sense a sudden happiness in them instead, something attained and enshrined out there in the Adirondack chairs. They believe this happiness will be theirs too, when they grow up.

Summer houses are the last WASP outposts of johnny-cake breakfasts and cold-water plunges; houses that were built as desperate 19th-century attempts to hold onto strengths and virtues that only remain now in the attic as ghosts hovering over old oars, a broken banjo and albums of sepia photographs glued to black paper with "corners" — pictures of men standing on a long-lost yawl, puffing out their chests; of a beefy cook and the feebleminded daughter she always claimed was her niece.

The no-longer-so-rich families try to keep them going out of a mysterious sense of noblesse oblige — but oblige to what or whom? As years go by, the winters come to be full of phone calls debating a new roof, and is there

Chebeague boatyard (drawing by the author).

any sense in trying to fix the sailboat? And what with the taxes and the burglary last winter, wouldn't it be easier to sell the place? The anguish! Whole childhoods will vanish, along with the ultimate promise of a summer house — that it will always be there to redeem the gray dwindlings of modern life. But ultimately, it goes on the market. And no one in the whole family has the money to buy it.

What happened to their strength, their virtue and, oh, their money?

Summer houses are where: You see a copperhead behind the springhouse and feel the whole world go hard, wise, and dark on you as you back away from it. You lie awake listening to the weather-vane goose spin its wings in the dark. You vow that this time you will not turn back into a ghost of yourself when you get back to the city, even though you know you have vowed this before. You compete to see who can imitate the local accent best. You roll up a straw rug to sweep, and you see perfect little rows of sand. You will remember the feel of the lawn — bristly, because you always walked on it barefoot. You will remember the smell of the house — a combination of mothballs, caramel, pine trees, citronella, and the faint vegetable breath of that slow sink drain with its brass screen.

You go to the inn for dinner.

"We eat here every summer," your sister says to the waitress. "And I always have a milkshake."

"That's nice, hon," the waitress says. "What flavor you want this year?"

Ah, the locals. Kind as they may be, there is a tightening in their eyes when they see you have taken the romance of the summer house so far that you believe you belong to this place, that you spend 11 months of the year somewhere else but you live here.

You say: "Someday, I want to winter over here. It must be beautiful."

They say: "Maybe so. I spend as much of it as I can in Florida."

The locals keep breaking the faith — building condominiums or putting a neon sign on the store. Even if you own property, you can't stop them because the town meetings are held over the winter when you aren't there. Sometimes their children go off to college and end up living in the Unreal City, and in a voice carefully modulated to avoid condescension, you congratulate them. But you are sick at heart. Don't they understand?

As it happens, they ask the same question about you.

There is often an offspring of a rich family, usually a boy, who flounders for a while in the city and then asks to try living in the summer house year-round, and be a carpenter, a fisherman, a potter. This is very romantic. It is also a symptom of the disease known in the Northeast as "WASP Rot." If he sticks it out, the whole winter, with the pipes freezing, the wires down in the blizzard, the chainsaw broken, the locals will look at him come spring with grudging acceptance and think: "His family must be disappointed in him."

Summer houses are where you believe you are who you are and the world is what it is, but you have to leave.

The last morning comes. It is always the same. Breakfast

is no good. The dog runs away. Down at the store there is a goodbye said to a lifeguard, a goodbye accompanied by lifted eyebrows and a request for communication — by letter, e-mail, text, tweet. It doesn't matter because it won't happen anyway.

You stack the newspapers by the fireplace. You look at your photographs, knowing that they'll puzzle you yet again with their pallid failure to limn the sunset after the thunderstorm, or the potato race at Old Home Day. You note with regret that you never watered the front-walk petunias — this omission somehow shows you don't have as much claim on this place as you'd hoped. Did you pack your dress shoes? Your copy of *Anna Karenina*?

The dog is found. The woman from the village arrives to clean.

"We hate to leave," you say.

"You've had nice weather," she says. "Right up till today."

"Oh, we have. But this morning the radio said thunderstorms."

"I'll close all the windows," she says.

My father on the conning tower of the LCI 1091.

United States Navy
LCI 1091

. . . four kamikazes came in at sunset . . .

This was in the dining room at Fanwood, at three o'clock on a Sunday afternoon, April 26, 1953, the first day of daylight savings time, as it happened, with its slightly dislocated feeling.

French horns sprang out of our 12-inch black-and-white RCA television. On the screen, black-and-white ocean rolled behind the title: *Victory at Sea*. This was the second to last of 26 episodes about the Navy in World War II.

My father had been waiting for this episode since the series began in October. It was called "Suicide for Glory" and it was about the massive, months-long steel-sky death match between the Navy and the kamikazes at Okinawa. The Navy had more men killed than either the Army or the Marine Corps lost on land.

Okinawa was Dad's battle, 82 days of it fought from his

ship, the *LCI (L) 1091*, Lt. Henry S. Allen, commanding. *LCI* stood for landing craft infantry and *L* for large. It wasn't a big ship — 158 feet long — but it was his ship and he was my father.

I had been watching *Victory at Sea* with him every week, and, just as important, I had watched him watch it. We both waited for spring, and the last battle of the war, Okinawa. Now, in his usual TV-watching position, he lay back on a day bed in our dining room, his head resting against wallpaper that bore a grease spot from the Vitalis he used on his hair. The French horns sounded, the ocean rolled.

The episode began with an odd evocation of the cherry-blossom aesthetics of Japan, carp in ponds with lovely bridges, that kind of travelogue thing. With the same ritual grace, kamikaze pilots toasted each other and climbed into their planes to die. The point was that next to this beauty lurked bringers of chaos, a mass suicidal ferocity, a culture in which suicide could be a way not just of death but of life.

Next appeared the big American ships, the battleships not so much cutting as insisting their wide way through the waves, 40 aircraft carriers, 200 destroyers, 1300 ships in all, the *LCI 1091* being one of them.

Then the kamikazes coming out of the sun, American planes trying to shoot them down before they could hit our ships, anti-aircraft guns pumping millions of shells into the sky.

An old-school Princeton gentleman, my father disdained shows of emotion, but the Okinawa segment undid him. His face seemed to tighten — his war face, his command face.

The planes came in toward the cameras, endless kamikazes twitching through anti-aircraft fire. He rose halfway from the couch, pointing and shouting: "Get him! Get him! Starboard bow, get him! Get him!"

I was startled, even alarmed. I knew better than to ask him about it.

Now, more than 60 years later, a photograph of the *1091* hangs on a wall of my studio, a gray and dirty combat ship pushing against a bow wave, looking tired on a cloudy day.

Hanging next to the photograph are a souvenir samurai sword, a tatter of the *1091's* long, thin commissioning pennant, and my father's ribbons — a shrine to a lost era of Americans fighting in not just a worthy cause but a victorious one.

A year after he'd seen the waters around the *1091* heaving with corpses, I watched my father extract the photograph from a mailing tube in our living room. He unrolled it on a table. I sensed even then that he saw things in it that my mother and I could not. I was told not to touch it.

Dad framed the picture. It travelled with us from house to house.

He told me stories about the *1091*, but only the funny ones, like the one about the crewman who liked to start fights with Coast Guardsmen he called the "teacup navy."

Later he told me about taking the *1091* from the shipyard in Bay City, Michigan, in 1943, down the Great Lakes to the Chicago River and finally out to the Mississippi where he saw country women sitting on the banks nursing babies — a starchy Yankee, he was shocked. Then through the Panama Canal to California, then stops at Hawaii, Guam, and Eniwetok on the way to Iwo Jima, where he arrived toward the end of the battle and was ordered to keep on going to the next one, Okinawa. Soon he would watch Marines with flamethrowers moving like postmen from cave to cave. He saw some of the thousands of Japanese civilians who jumped to their deaths from cliffs at the end of the battle.

"Women with babies in their arms," he said.

He died in 1982, already senile at the age of 71, and I inherited all his pictures of the *1091* and its crew, a briefcase full of orders and the navigation charts of Okinawa he'd inscribed with a pencil and a straight-edge.

On the back of a picture of his crew in dress blues he had quoted Tennyson in pencil:

> My mariners,
> Souls that have toil'd, and wrought, and thought with me —
> That ever with a frolic welcome took
> The thunder and the sunshine, and opposed
> Free hearts, free foreheads . . .

One night in 2001 I was in the shower, where I do some of my best thinking. I realized that if my father's *LCI* was numbered *1091*, there must have been a lot of them, and a lot of sailors who sailed on them.

I dried off, headed for my computer, and punched Landing Craft Infantry into one of the new search engines on the internet, the long gone *Alta Vista*, I think. Sure enough, there were enough *LCI* sailors to hold conventions and run a newsletter. I thought of how proud and happy my father would have been to know this.

The next night, on a wild off-chance I tried punching in *LCI 1091*.

What I saw brought me out of my chair, my chair spinning backwards and my blood rushing as I went blind with excitement and shouted to my wife: "I found my father's ship! I found the *1091*! I have found it."

Of all the *LCIs* built in all the world the only one intact then was my father's and it was in Eureka, Calif., owned by a dentist named Ralph Davis who was restoring it to World War II condition. I found my father's ship. Somehow, in a way that brings tears to my eyes even now, my father was redeemed and I, in my boyhood dreams, was justified. Dad! Dad! I found your ship! I found the *1091*!

I learned more history of the *1091*. After a stint at the Bikini atoll atom bomb tests, and landings in the north during the Korean War to see if there was bubonic plague there (there was smallpox instead), the *1091* came home to Astoria, Ore., to be sold to a fishing company that used it for 20 years on the Yukon River.

In 1989, Davis bought it. I called him. He knew nothing of the ship's early history. We arranged for my elder son Peter and me to fly out there from Washington, D.C., in August. I would bring photographs, carbon copies of old orders, souvenirs.

I made more calls, sent more messages. I found a quartermaster named Loyel "Bud" Hoseck. He'd spent the battle of Okinawa standing on the conning tower with my father, working signals. Now he was retired in Minnesota. He told me stories my father had not.

"The first night we got to Okinawa four kamikazes came in at sunset, coming so close you could almost touch them," he said. "The battleship *Missouri* was a block away. A kamikaze hit it, there were 41 killed."

He'd kept a diary, and written a brief memoir. He sent them to me. They told of fears of torpedo boats and suicide barges, of the *1091* having to shoot up boxes and crates on the chance they might be bombs propelled by suicide swimmers; how they threw away bad mutton and chicken from Australia and lived on little but macaroni and cheese instead, a diet so tedious that K-rations were a treat. They had a phonograph, but only one record: "Don't Fence Me In."

> May 12, 1945: *LCI* blown up by suicide plane, two survivors. Planes strafed and killed engineering officer and two men on *LSM-414.* Had been moored alongside them the day before. Suicide plane crashed into New Mexico, killed about 150 men. I saw it come in at dusk, out of sun.
>
> May 28, 1945: Low flying Jap plane blown up right off our starboard bow. My birthday and a lonely one. *LCI* hit.
>
> June 24, 1945: Close shave with death. An *APD* was hit by a Jap suicide plane. We were to escort her to Ie Shima but our

> orders were changed at the last minute and an *LSM* and an
> *LCS* took our place. Three Jap suicide planes came in low,
> radar failed to pick them up. Sunk all three ships, just a few
> survivors. Lucky our orders were changed.

And then there's the laconic entry of a combat-weary sailor
who is well past making a big deal out of anything.

> August 6, 1945: A-bomb Hiroshima. Mail run. Got several
> letters.

In more than a year, they spent only two or three days
off the ship. One of the first places they landed after the battle was Nagasaki. I asked my father what it looked like.

"There was nothing there," he said.

In August, my son Peter and I flew to Eureka.

It turned out to be a faded lumber and fishing town
stranded 280 miles north of San Francisco, full of Victorian
houses from the great timbering days and so far north that
Route 101 has turned into a two-lane road. The ocean is so
cold and the air so dank the beaches are always empty. It had
the feeling of a museum of lost eras, a relic decorated with its
heyday's houses, and hippies who hadn't changed for 30
years, still with their VW microbuses and a baffled marijuana
lethargy.

Captain Ralph drove us down to the water the next morning, bumping through the scrub and rusty barbed wire fences of never-happen shoreline real-estate schemes. My first glance was over bushes and there was no doubt: the conning tower with mast and rigging.

"There she is," I said, stoked with a fury of excitement.

"That's right," said Captain Ralph.

She was tied to pilings in tidal flats. We came alongside in an outboard motor boat. Up a ladder and then the impossible was possible, the legendary real, the past redeemed, my father's ship reclaimed.

Like other Navy ships I've been on, it was impersonal and cozy at the same time, rivets and beams, all gray paint — Navy ships have a way of looking like they're built of gray paint. Our feet rang on ladders, we smelled the eternal diesel smell, we saw marks on the deck where the guns had been. (*Get him! Get him!*)

In the galley we pictured the cook bracing against cabinets as he stirred batter with the storied baseball bat and the ship rocked — it was a landing ship and it only drew five feet of water, no keel to grip the water beneath the waves and keep it from lurching side-to-side.

We toured dim labyrinths of troop and crew compartments lit by bare bulbs, and I remembered the troop ships where I'd lain as a Marine on my rack — canvas strung between pipes — hearing the Pacific Ocean hiss past the steel plating.

My father's quarters, topside, had a porthole and a desk, the original. I imagined him scrambling out of his rack and up to the conning tower for yet another night attack, the crew racing to general quarters — sprinting up to the gun tubs in helmets, down to the dank sweat of a diesel-roaring engine room, while my father, with that face I'd seen in front of the television, peered into a night sky lit with dirty explosions, death, and the weirdly languid arcs of tracers.

Except now, of course, it was a cool and quiet morning in northern California.

My son and I posed for pictures on the conning tower ladder where my father stood a million years ago to have his picture taken too. Feeling both intensely alone and intensely scrutinized, I climbed to the conning tower and looked out over the bay. I said a prayer, nothing in particular, just a sort of offering to the gods of war, fathers, and memory.

In the years since 2001, the *1091* has become a museum moored in downtown Eureka, a tourist attraction. It serves meals cooked in the galley and ladled onto mess trays. It has a dues-paying membership association.

My son Peter and I pose in front of the LCI 1091 conning tower.

"I brought the original commissioning pennant," I say to Captain Ralph.

"Let's run it up," he says.

It's faded now, a long thin thing with seven stars and two stripes, red and white. With rare exceptions, one flies from the mast of every American warship, a Navy ritual. This one flew when the ship powered out of the yard in Michigan, my father in command.

We hoisted it, along with the American flag. Symbolically or even technically, the pennant meant that the ship was my father's again, or so I chose to interpret Navy regulations at that moment.

I saluted.

Carnegie Hall, Hamilton College.

Hamilton College &
the Marine Corps

*. . . a vast wind could blow the college
off the hill in an instant . . .*

The American teenager was invented in the 1940s and perfected in the 1950s, fitted out with new and exhilarating entitlements including cars, private phones, rock and roll, and television, all unknown to a previous generation. We took them for granted.

At the same time, some of us among the college-bound felt a fierce nostalgia for the '20s and '30s, Hemingway and Fitzgerald, speakeasies, the cultivated cynicism of the Algonquin Round Table, college students as culture heroes, the Spanish Civil War, all laden with a meaning that seemed to have evaporated in the Eisenhower years. Nostalgia is an affliction of the young more than the old, I think. In any case, it served to give us respect for our parents' youth, and for the bastion of tradition that was college.

Off I went in 1959 to live for four years at Hamilton, a

college of 800 men on a hilltop in Clinton, N.Y. with a campus studded with noble trees and an all-American jumble of architecture — the Gothic library, the bulky neo-classicism of Root Hall, the brown bunker called Carnegie dormitory, the gothic arches of South dormitory and the casement-windowed Tudor of the Sigma Phi house.

We found ourselves stripped of our teenage entitlements but glad of it, at first — anachronism has an authenticity about it. We accepted the ban on cars for freshmen and sophomores. The ordained ethos seemed to hark back to some halcyon 1938 or so, when Hamilton believed itself to be a tiny Oxford, a cloister preserving civilization and a modest aristocracy in the steppes of upstate. This belief had made Hamilton complacent over the years, the sort of college where professors wrote no books, never changed their courses and had cute nicknames: Swampy Marsh, Noah Count, Digger Graves. Rumor had it that one legacy student had his father's notes from the 18th century literature course taught for decades by the same professor, and they still worked just fine.

The past ruled as if by divine right. There were time-warp oddities such as the sanctioned hazing of freshmen. We were ordered to wear beanies, for instance, and to run a gauntlet every Tuesday after the campus meeting in the chapel. We filed out and the members of a sophomore cool-guy society — DT? Was Los? — would seize someone who had neglected to wear his beanie and humiliate him by hanging a toilet seat around his neck and ordering him to wear it all day.

Under threat of expulsion, we attended Sunday night chapel services. We had to wear jackets and ties to dinner. We could cut classes three times in a semester. Hamilton seemed like a boarding school with beer.

Lurking beneath Hamilton's complacency was an inferiority complex. Had it always been there, or had it arisen as upstate New York declined and New England revived?

We knew we lacked the prestige of New England's Little Three — Amherst, Wesleyan, and Williams — but we thought of ourselves as a big cut above nearby Hobart and Colgate. Tom Wolfe once referred to Hamilton as "threadneedle Ivy," after the heavy-soled faculty shoes also known as "corridor creepers."

I remember staring out a window one day and sensing that a vast wind could blow the college off the hill in an instant, that it could vanish as if had never been there. This thought gave Hamilton a liminal feeling to me, liminal in the

ʌropologist's sense of straddling realities, neither fish nor
owl. Indeed, Midwesterners thought of Hamilton as Eastern. New Englanders thought of it as Midwestern.

Those who came from New York State were less puzzled. They had grown up in the upstate where Hamilton
hung onto its standing by providing big frogs for small
ponds — pediatricians or bank vice presidents in Skaneateles
or Olean or Glens Falls.

The administration insisted that Hamilton's archrival was
Union, a college in Schenectady that no one cared about. It
no doubt had meant something in the world when upstate
was a culture unto itself, with its factories and progress.

The miracle of photography from Rochester! Mark Twain
in Elmira, Edmund Wilson and Mary McCarthy in Tal-
cottville! Utica's radio factory and tool-and-die works!
Black skies and full lunch pails! Schenectady's General Electric, where progress was the most important product! But by
1959 Union was even less famous than Hamilton and the
progress franchise had moved to California.

Now, Utica, a bus ride away, felt like a ghost town full of
people. There was a string of gay bars — why in Utica? —
and the Lafayette Show Bar where high-collared Mafia
wiseguys ignored the strippers. *Time* magazine wrote: "If

you want to kill somebody go to Utica, but don't double park."

Anyway, we were supposed to care deeply about the football game with Union, and share the enthusiasm of Dean Winton Tolles up in the top row of the bleachers. He'd sip attentively at a thermos and bellow "Go Blue!" so loudly that he embarrassed us. He was said to be a great man. No one said why. "Great Man" was his assigned role in the Hamilton pageant.

There were signs of hipness — echoes of Greenwich Village or San Francisco's North Beach. Portable phonographs played Dave Brubeck's "Take Five" over and over. Gloomy beards were grown and sandals were worn at the Emerson Literary Society, a fraternity that was home to a lot of the Jews on campus. A film society, founded a year or two later, would name itself "Kinokunst Gesellschaft."

For some of us, first in our families to go to college, it was a chance to prospect for the gold of the American dream. For others, it was a chance to play sports, indulge intellectual passions or get into medical school.

For still others, many others, it was a rowdy Round Table our fathers had known and we had read about in F. Scott Fitzgerald, Evelyn Waugh, James Joyce, and J.P. Donleavy. Had they needed cars? Girls? Television? Of course not, so why did we? Some of us would even re-enact legends from our fathers' college days, the '20s and '30s, going down to Clinton Village to buy cider that would harden into alcohol, as if Prohibition had never ended. (The cider turned to vinegar and a muck called "mother.")

We envied tales of pranks played long ago — the cow in the chapel steeple, hippopotamus footprints made in the snow with an umbrella stand. Oddly, we never came up with any of our own, unless you count one classmate breaking into the chapel to lay his penis on the altar and dare God to strike him dead. (God didn't get around to it until 2002.)

There was little to do for social life except to walk down the hill and drink at the Village Tavern, the Park Hotel or Alteri's, the drinking age being 18 then. Then we'd walk back up the hill. Other amusements of freshman year included vomiting, masturbation and playing lacrosse in the hallways of Dunham dormitory, "that triumph of economics over the imagination" said one professor.

There were still scions of gentry with their tweed sport coats and deb party invitations, but they were losing ground to the scions of rock and roll, which had transformed young white America only five years before and created a new generation that wore Levis and admired vandalism. Cultural interbreeding produced students who wore tweed sport coats with Levis and would later turn vandalism into a house party ritual, burning cars at Chi Psi and pushing a grand piano off a porch at Psi U.

I joined Sigma Phi. We wore tuxedos at house parties and forbade the wearing of white socks at dinner. We had the lowest marks of any fraternity and probably the fewest varsity athletes. We were above all that. Irony, an easy substitute for meaning, filled the air like swamp gas. Later, Sigma Phi's own trustees closed it for four years to expunge what was called "an alien subculture."

I fit in there — neither scholar nor athlete, just a preppy slacker bohemian spending my time wanting to be a writer but not doing any writing. I did nothing to save myself from profound and perverse depression. I listened to modern jazz and read far more off the curriculum than on it. (Chekhov! Waugh! Faulkner!)

Campus celebrities known as "hot shits" awed us. They were often personalities of the sort that Fitzgerald was talking about when he described college men "who reach such an acute limited excellence at twenty-one that everything afterward savors of anti-climax." I was not one of them. I felt despised, in fact, but I would like to think that was mostly the depression talking. I wasn't prominent enough to be despised.

There was the occasional glamorous faculty member such as Jascha Kessler who published short stories and poetry but he soon left. There were the nervous cheekbones of Professor Austin Briggs's beautiful wife. Not having seen a female for weeks at a time (except for the cleaning women we called "harpies"), we would stare at her, even dream about her.

Charismatic John Baldwin led the choir and played the organ with bright-eyed, pink-cheeked rapture that argued well for the amount of drinking that was customary. One suspected that a tip-serve half-gallon whiskey caddy stood on every faculty sideboard.

There was a sense of something skewed about the place, perhaps a feeling that we were being asked to live up to something that may never have existed.

One night I heard the chaplain, a fierce and glaring Scot, explain it this way: "Hamilton is everyone's second choice."

But there we were, doing our best to pretend it wasn't. We were helped by the fact that the first-rate part of Hamilton revealed itself instantly and totally to incoming freshmen

— a curriculum that was an intellectual boot camp designed to show us we were as yet unable to write, read, think, or be worthy in any way of the civilization we were supposed to inherit.

The author at 19.

Our English composition themes came back littered with elegant sarcasms: "Do tell," or "One trembles!" Freshman biology hammered the sentiment out of us and hammered the scientific method in. In the freshman history course we scoffed when Digger Graves and company handed out blank maps and asked us to mark the locations of various world capitals. Hadn't we learned that in junior high school? When the maps were handed back we saw we'd confused Ireland with Iceland and misplaced Moscow by 1100 miles.

We were challenged. We responded. And those who didn't respond to the challenge of writing three perfect one-page English papers were threatened with expulsion at the end of the first semester. Something was at stake beyond today's self-esteem and identity entitlements. The faculty didn't care how we felt, they only cared what we did. Except for a few flunk-outs, the system produced confidence and competence and we were — and are — the better for it.

Nowadays, under the "open curriculum," there are no required courses at all — a situation that may well have contributed to the vast numbers of applications Hamilton gets every year.

As an already white Christmas approached in my first semester, we were promised the wonders of a reading to be given in the chapel by a retired and revered English professor named Robert "Bobo" Rudd, Class of '09.

Frail and white-haired, Professor Rudd tottered toward the lectern and began to speak in a slurred rasp. Was he having a stroke? I was relieved to realize he was merely drunk. Later that night I saw him standing in the snow in front of Dunham, even drunker. Faculty members restrained him from storming into the place — his intentions had something to do with the way he kept waving his arms and screaming: "There's a lot of cock up there!"

This incident was ignored like other Bobo squalors until it was forgotten. Hamilton needed all the myths it could get, and Bobo was one of them. What corporation or legislature, country club or bowling alley would have put up with this? Perhaps the lesson was that Hamilton was above that world, maybe above any world but itself.

We soothed our doubts about Hamilton's rank by reciting a litany of famous alumni such as the drama critic Alexander Woolcott, who was quoted frequently as saying that Hamilton was a small place, but there are those who love it. As it happened, it was Daniel Webster who had said that about Dartmouth in 1819.

There was B.F. Skinner, a father of then-fashionable behavioral psychology, noted for raising his child in a box and teaching pigeons to play pingpong. There was Sol Linowitz, head of Xerox and an ambassador. Jewish, he was said to have had a lonely existence at Hamilton, and even in our time a persistent anti-Semitism limited the Jews in certain fraternities. Any black student was always in danger of being elected class president.

Ezra Pound '05 was a giant of 20th century literature, but he was also a fascist loon and traitor and he was scarcely mentioned in English classes. Though a statue of Alexander Hamilton stood on the campus, I never heard anyone talk about him either. What had he done wrong? Now, much is made of him, though his politics opposed the leftism that pervades the faculty now.

Elihu Root, Hamilton 1864, had been secretary of state under Teddy Roosevelt and sometimes one could see his descendants wandering around Clinton with the preoccupied air of aristocrats who know they're failing at something but aren't sure what. There were a number of families of that sort in Clinton.

By senior year, my depression had turned into a panic. I saw a future for myself not as a writer but as an alcoholic ad-agency type who at 45 would have three ex-wives and a col-

Marine Corps, 1966.

lection of children who wouldn't speak to me.

And so, in my madness, I made the first great decision of my life: I would quit Hamilton and everything it summed up in my life and enlist in the Marine Corps. A little like my father leaving Princeton to sail the Atlantic. It made no sense to anyone, but I never doubted myself. It was my last chance to avoid the slacker disgrace that loomed as my fate, to reject gentility as a life ambition, to keep from ending up as nobody. I knew then as I know now that if you have been a Marine, you are somebody.

We don't need another description of Marine boot camp, the drill instructors with campaign hats tilted forward in an azimuth of aggression, their barking strut, the mind-scrambling shouting . . . Do we?

And who cares about the drab horizontal world of barracks and drill fields known as grinders . . . of indignities — skidding on vomit in the berthing compartments of troop ships . . . the small-hours pecker checks for gonorrhea . . . whores . . . the exquisite hierarchies . . . I remember when both sergeants and corporals were allowed to hang curtains across the front of their cubicles in Okinawa until the sergeants complained: if the corporals had curtains, then the sergeants would have no privilege, so the corporals had to take their curtains down.

Yet you were a Marine. No matter how much failure, madness or addiction in your life, or how much triumph, achievement or freedom, you could sum it all up, then say, along with the actor Lee Marvin, who was wounded on Saipan during World War II, and later won an Oscar: "And, by God, I was a Marine."

Marines of my day, half a century ago, cultivated a tight-lipped, tight-eyed, full-body flex, a look of outraged intention. There was beauty — a platoon drilling on the grinder, close-order drill, a dance of order defying the god of combat, which is Chaos . . . the division band pumping out the Marine Corps Hymn as they passed in review. Taps playing as the flag slowly came down at sunset.

Marines do not expect to be understood — a Southern combination of politeness and entitlement, a mystique founded on a willful and even perverse modesty.

Not the modesty of Spartans, kamikazes or the French Foreign Legion parading at a half-time funeral step with leather aprons and axes, but a pristine and hard-eyed dirt-farm stinginess, a nearly lost American poor-but-proud aesthetic that makes Marines enjoy their belief that they're always fighting with hand-me-down equipment and not enough troops (because one Marine is as good as ten of any enemy, a belief that was just as wrong and destructive when the Confederate army believed it, too).

There are also the extravagant casualties that provoke the Marine wisecrack that the corps is the finest machine ever developed for the killing of young American men. A friend of mine once heard a Marine colonel say to an Army colonel:

"The Army uses tanks to protect men. The Marines use men to protect tanks."

Carved into a stone wall at the National Museum of the Marine Corps are the words of Sgt. Maj. Dan Daly, twice a Medal of Honor winner: "Come on, you sons of bitches, do you want to live forever?"

This is the point where courage becomes irony. If you cannot savor this sort of irony and understand that it is irony, the Marine mystique will elude you. But like a beautiful woman, the Marine Corps is secretly delighted to think that you don't understand it. Beyond that, it doesn't give a damn.

The Marine Corps has a sub-cadre of interesting people, eccentrics with interesting tastes in reading. I read more there than I'd read in college. I discovered existentialism on a troopship heading for Vietnam. Every day I sat on the deck next to staff sergeants playing pinochle while I read Sartre and Dostoyevsky about absurdity, decision, transcendence, and meaning. Existentialism seemed to apply in Vietnam, a grim business I had to take care of without knowing precisely why, except to the extent that I'd read every book I could find about Vietnam, French Indochina, and an ancient culture founded on the glory of repelling invaders, starting with the leadership of the Trung sisters in the first century A.D.

I read them in part because I knew I would be asked about Vietnam when I returned to Hamilton, and surely people would want to know.

People did not want to know. They wanted to lecture me about Vietnam, lectures backed up by a careful reading of *The New York Times*.

When I visited the dean, the much-respected Winton Tolles, to request reinstatement, he said only: "You're in." He asked me nothing about Vietnam or the Marine Corps, though he complained about Korean War veterans who had refused to put up with rules they found ridiculous.

Later, in an October twilight, the Asian history professor stopped me on the quadrangle and asked me three questions about Vietnam, then excused himself. It seemed he was late for dinner. I was a strange, intense combat veteran stalking the apathetic and parochial campus where no student spoke to me for five weeks. No one lacks curiosity like college students. Later, I befriended other drop-outs, and at a prize day the following June I had the pleasure of hearing my classmates whisper to each other "Who the hell is Henry Allen?" when my name was announced as winner of the American Academy of Poets Prize, a nice $300 that paid my first three months' rent on an apartment in Manhattan where I went to work at the *New York Daily News*.

The final delight of Hamilton, the perfect irony, was opening my yearbook and discovering that the editors had interchanged me with someone I'd never heard of, one Ralph Durwood Almkuist II — his picture was over my name, and my picture over his. I tore the page out and framed it.

Lake house in Michigan.

Brief Stops

We were poor, we were rich.

lived in a tent in the endless rain in the Sangre de Cristo mountains of New Mexico. I lived in a hotel room in a fishing village in Crete. Both my sister Julie and I lived in a collection of apartments with the provisional Manhattan quality that reminds you that you are no more than an item in a rent-paying aggregate, that you are fungible, and the apartment is the real citizen of New York.

As the late '60s turned into the sluggish disorder of the '70s, my parents moved from rental to rental north of New Haven, my mother hissing, "I hate living in a rented house." In one, burglars took my father's war souvenirs, and his mother's sterling silver tea set. For him it was as if they'd cut out the beating heart of his family, and so, broke as he was, he used the insurance money to buy another tea set, not sterling, alas, but plate. It was a symbol, all the more symbolic in its uselessness.

After her divorce my sister bought a townhouse in Fairfield, Conn., with a commons in back and a supermarket in front. She raised two children there.

I shared a floor-through loft in Washington with two artists, Bob Stark and Lucy Clark. It had one light and one radiator that used to serve as a subwoofer for the jukebox in the Benbow, the legendarily funky bar on the first floor — I can still sing the entire bass line of George Harrison's "My Sweet Lord." Bob and Lucy held a show of their work in the loft. At the last minute they saw that the stove was a crusty, dented wreck so they threw it out the window and after that we cooked with a toaster oven — a diet largely of lentils, with the occasional festive hot dog chunk thrown in.

We were poor, we were rich. Our rent was $75 a month for all of us. Then, on Nov. 8, 1970, I got a job as a copyeditor at *The Washington Post* and was richer even than I'd been when covering the White House for the *New York Daily News*.

One more Dupont Circle apartment later, I'd met Deborah. She dropped out of the University of Texas to live there until she found us a tiny one-bedroom house on a

Maryland bluff over the Potomac. The tile floors were damp from river humidity all summer, planes from National Airport shook the place like the subwoofer radiator in the loft. In back of us was a ravine. One morning Deborah awoke to hear a man on our back terrace shouting, "It's God's garden! It's God's garden." He was naked. No doubt lost in the sizzling clarity of LSD, he leapt off the terrace and ran away through the woods.

We had a daughter, Hannah Rose. I was so excited that I didn't sleep for 36 hours. Next we rented a scuffed-up center-hall colonial in Bethesda, then sublet that for nine months when I had a fellowship at the University of Michigan.

There we lived on a lake surrounded by ramshackle little houses ten miles north of Ann Arbor. The lake froze clear. Skating on it was like flying over beer cans and the occasional small-mouth bass. One day a crack flashed under my skates like a crack in the sky, a clean, perfect and menacing LSD feeling about it, but the ice didn't collapse beneath me.

The house was a tiny, semi-winterized summer cottage. Our daughter Hannah was a thrillingly beautiful three. Until big snow came, we'd skate on the lake while she pretended to skate in her little red sneakers. It was a fine year.

It was also my most enlightening year since the reading

I did in the Marine Corps. I'd gotten interested in Gregory Bateson, a biologist/anthropologist who wrote about information theory, as we called it then. He said: "Information is a difference that makes a difference."

This was as gnomic a doctrine as I'd encountered since Marshall McLuhan said, "The electric light is pure information."

I thought about it. The line reminded me of the old news saying: "When a dog bites a man, that is not news, because it happens so often. But if a man bites a dog, that is news."

It was anthropologists at Michigan who were hip to Bateson, so I hung out with them.

They steered me to Roland Barthes, the French semiologist who understood the importance of meaning in everyday life — professional wrestling, Greta Garbo's face, detergents, plastic. Years later at the University of Maryland, I would teach a course called "What Things Mean" and at *The Washington Post* I wrote about the meaning of plastic.

I learned that there is something but not a lot to be learned from deconstruction, or any of the other frenzied yet smug abstractions of French intellectuals. All I remember from Jean Baudrillard's *America* was his line about Santa Barbara's "picture windows like Snow White's glass coffin."

I never considered buying a house back then. I couldn't imagine anything but the nomadic life I'd been living. My parents and my sister kept moving too. This instability seemed appropriate at the time. Those were years that were over-sharpened to a feather-edge by drugs and the lies of Vietnam, sexual revolution, polemics, and manifestos, Watergate, paranoia, and the American dream that was like something packed in cardboard boxes for a move to a future that would never come.

Then our first son, Peter, arrived and I saw that the future was here and it looked nothing like the blown-mind liberation I had imagined, there were things more important than the American dream and it was time to buy a house.

Downtown Takoma Park (drawing by the author).

Takoma Park

. . . the dental-floss underground . . .

When we moved to Takoma Park, Md. in 1977 —
Deborah, Hannah, Peter, and I (Nicholas was yet
to come) — it was a shabby little town of chain-link fences
and tire swings hanging from oak trees. People liked it that
way. It was a town where you called the druggist "Doc" and
the downtown skyline was full of phone wires, like in February or in an old photograph, the kind of photograph that
makes you wonder why somebody took it.

World War II lingered in illegal apartments with buckled
beaverboard walls and crusty stoves. Government workers
had lived in them once. Now it was single mothers, failed
astrologers, revolutionaries, marijuana dealers, and an
assortment of would-be has-beens building a new world out
of lentils and Indian bedspreads. Rented rooms sheltered

alcoholic ex-taxi drivers who had the ghastly mildness of people wanting to be left alone, teetering indefinitely on whatever brink felt most like home.

In the late '40s, the greatest salesman in the history of asbestos had come through town like the Johnny Appleseed of fireproof siding, leaving behind house after house shrouded in quiet, chemical colors that sucked the light in and never let it go — a reason people called it "Tacky Park." Feral shrubbery climbed over old people's houses that were museums of lost air, the smell of 1948, ancient hair tonic, and a long-gone dog on their furniture. There were lots of old people, which is why the town also got called "Glaucoma Park." In their backyards were ghosts of overgrown goldfish ponds and sundial gardens.

We didn't move there in spite of this stuff, we moved there because of it. Washington is the city for people who don't like cities, and Takoma Park in 1977 was the suburb for people who didn't like suburbs. Also, we could afford it, not on a *Washington Post* salary, but once, by God, I was a Marine, and the prize at the bottom of that particular Cracker Jack box was a VA mortgage. And my wife Deborah could stay home to take care of the kids in defiance of the fashionable feminism of those years.

For $60,000 we bought an asbestos-sided American foursquare, 30 by 30 feet, painted army green with a metal pyramid roof and a quarter acre of land where grass had made attempts to grow.

It stank of cat pee. The seller was a cat breeder with 35 Persians she said she kept caged in the basement. She didn't. When I tore up her 1970s shag rugs, cat pee ran off my elbows. We sanded the floors but still on humid summer nights we smelled those Persians in the pantry until we replaced the cabinets and the flooring. Other '70s touches: cedar shingles on the walls of the kitchen, and glossy opium-poppy wallpaper on the ceiling of the dining room.

No air conditioning, and in the winter an oil furnace labored to fill the radiators with hot water. Two bedrooms and a sewing room. My wife and I slept on a mattress on the floor — our years in bohemia served us in good stead. Our daughter Hannah and our son Peter slept in bunk beds in the back bedroom. When Nicholas was born in 1980 we turned the attic into a bedroom.

My mother shuddered at the place. After my father died in 1982, we moved her into a county-supported studio apartment in downtown Takoma. After she'd lived there for a while — she stayed for 15 years — it stank of Merit cigarettes and the kitchen floor was scabby with dirt — she refused to let me hire a cleaner. One Sunday, as I brought her back from a drive in the country, she said: "If I'd known I was going to end up like this, I'd have slit my throat."

I don't think she was blaming me — she'd already established my willful failure to achieve gentility. I accepted the stingy paychecks of *The Washington Post* in exchange for writing what I wanted. She hated my wife, a Jewish woman from no money at all. She disliked two of my children. She liked my middle child, Peter, though. One day, while bicycling he and I were talking and I burst out laughing at the sudden thought that she liked Peter better than me.

When she died, Peter and I took her ashes to a pond in New Hampshire where she had spent happy girlhood summers with Aunt Fan and Uncle Fult. We rowed around until the spot seemed right and we emptied the urn.

Driving away, we got near that spot and I heard her voice, using my boyhood name. It said: "Thanks, Ren."

As for me, I was happy in Takoma Park. Something about it, maybe the starter home atmosphere, reminded me a little of the Fanwood I'd grown up in.

Takoma Park in 1977 liked to call itself a typical American small town, one with a social structure built around the peace committee, the absentee landlord, the potluck supper, and a Fourth of July parade that never took less than an hour to go past. It felt like a 16,000-person in-joke. With a west wind, we had the heavenly smell of bread baking at the Giant bakery across the tracks. (A local environmentalist complained it was air pollution.) Like a lot of Maryland, it had the feeling of a no-man's land between North and South, strident Yankee moralism and self-entitled Southern eccentricities.

It had many identities, a lot of them mistaken.

"Goldie Hawn comes back here, but she doesn't tell anybody," the late Larry Mack told me of the movie star one day. He lived in a bungalow down the street from me. He was a retired steamfitter who spent winters listening to his police radio and summers sitting on his front porch. He'd lived there when Goldie Hawn was growing up two blocks away, dreaming of Hollywood.

"I was sitting out here last year, maybe two years ago, I saw her come past, walking down the sidewalk," Larry said. "She was wearing some kind of disguise so people wouldn't recognize her, but I recognized her. I said, 'Hey, Goldie!' She didn't even look up, she's an actress, you see, she wouldn't let it show. I said, 'Hey, Goldie! You think I don't recognize you? It's me, Larry Mack. I watched you running up and down that sidewalk when you were a little girl.' She never batted an eye, just kept on walking. She didn't want to be recognized."

Larry lived next to the group house where one of the group used to beat up his girlfriend on the front lawn on Friday nights. Nobody paid much attention. Word had it that they were dealing drugs. One night five guys from D.C. walked in with a submachine gun and tied everybody up for reasons that never became clear. Nobody was hurt, but when it was all over, the group decided to get friendlier with the police.

As it happened, our house had been robbed the week before, and the cops were coming by to hold a burglary prevention seminar in my living room. Two of the group decided to attend, but they got the address wrong, and knocked at the house next door.

"We're here for the meeting," they said.

My neighbor thought it was a little odd, but she let them in. It took them 20 minutes to figure out that the reason everybody was talking about sore nipples instead of deadbolts was that they'd wandered into a meeting of breastfeeding advocates in the La Leche League. Two days later they all moved out, leaving behind their used needles.

We had many eccentric philosophers. They claimed the perquisites of exiles from one thing or another, but as time went along and their various utopias were not accomplished, they came to seem simply stranded, trapped in some mid-larval stage, progressive and nostalgic at the same time. Takoma Park was famous for them: the government lawyers with their subscriptions to Maoist newsletters, holistic mid-wives, and subversive autoharpists, the Fruitarian Network telling people not to mow their lawns, the people who listened to them, apparently, until their houses were hidden in woods, and even a beatnik or two hanging on,

I walked into a Takoma Park poetry reading one night and heard a guy declaiming:

> Come dance the moist fandango!
> Come wallow in the mire!

Our son Peter, now a partner in law firm, played with two boys down the street, old-time Marylanders with the accent that pinches the O's and U's. They had a loaded pistol sitting on top of the refrigerator — the kind of household where you don't take the last beer. Citizens addressed the city council by singing folk songs. One council member sat through meetings looking like the Dormouse at the Mad

Hatter's Tea Party, waking only when somebody used the word "nuclear" — Takoma Park is a nuclear-free zone, and one of the few towns in America where illegal immigrants and 16-year-olds can vote, except, like most Parkies, they don't.

We had right-wingers too. One neighbor with a Pat Robertson for President sign on his lawn told me that Jesse Jackson's financing came from the Communist Party itself. A survivalist in back of us left for Wisconsin — he'd found land where he could generate his own hydroelectric power, which he couldn't with the little stream that divided our properties. (The stream did a fine job of moving old batteries downstream at a rate of 15 or 20 feet a year, however.) When he left he took the Civil War cannon that he used to fire in the general direction of my house every New Year's Eve. A bunch of us got together and bought another cannon to replace it.

There was the Dental Floss Underground. One night I had to talk to a neighbor about a problem he'd caused. I saw him in the street. I walked up to him. I started complaining, then saw the two-foot piece of dental floss hanging from his mouth. I gave up on the complaint. Another night I stopped to talk with a different neighbor, a research biologist who drove a car with a bumper sticker that said, "Think Legato." I may have been asking him what "Think Legato" meant when I noticed he had a two-foot length of dental floss hanging from *his* mouth. Were there more of these people?

Through the years we would turn the front yard desert into a garden, re-paint the house's dead army green with a warm gray, retrofit air-conditioning behind the crumbling plaster walls, replace the furnace, build a two-story addition with a tree growing through the roof, and pay off the mortgage. We sledded down the hill behind the junior high school. My kids played kickball in the street and chased fireflies. On the Fourth of July, I was called on to read aloud the Declaration of Independence at a picnic two doors down. We threw dinner parties that were un-Washingtonian in their disregard of rank and power — hilarious, ranting things that often concluded with skyrockets fired from the deck. Decorum returned when I quit drinking.

It was returning anyway as real estate prices soared by a factor of 15 since 1977. The semi-industrial, phone-wire, mid-Atlantic gloom lives on only in pockets. Big hippie dogs no longer run in packs. Ivy League decals appear in the back windows of cars. We've lost some racial mix and more class mix — the steamfitter living down the street from the assis-

Deborah (pastel portrait by the author).

tant secretary of state, the baker next to the botanist. I'm glad my children grew up with that — the worst segregation in America is between the classes.

Our house is a colorful, sheltering place where neighborhood kids used to come and play with ours. I wrote a novel or, I managed to write a novel, *Fool's Mercy*, in the sewing room. I stayed up very late reading in bed, doing obsessive research for my feature stories at the *Post*. In my late 50s, I called Deborah one Friday night and asked her to pick me up outside the *Post* immediately. She thought I'd had some crisis, and in a way I had. We drove up 15th St.

I said: "I've won the Pulitzer Prize."

She wept, instantly. I've seen her cry no more than five times.

"Why are you crying?" I asked.

"You've worked so hard," she said. It is the greatest compliment of my life. I had responded to the failures of some of my family with work that nearly destroyed my nervous

182

system. And we raised children in the house I like to call Fortress Takoma, children who have worked very hard and well. We care more about doing things than feeling things. My boast: I have three children with college degrees and no visible tattoos, and they all speak to me.

We have observed the rituals — Hanukah and beautiful Christmas trees with stockings we've hung by the chimney with care. At a recent Christmas, our three children and five grandchildren were here for days, no fighting, lots of laughing. In the late spring, a sea of Deborah's peonies reaches high tide in back of the house. Then come the lilies, hydrangeas, hostas,

Our children, Nicholas, Hannah, and Peter.

astilbe, butterfly bushes, and impatiens. Friends tell us we live in Eden. Our house is a very nice house, with much-loved, long-ago cats buried behind the azaleas. I nap in a hammock. The stream runs clear.

Things change, however. Newcomers don't make friends the way we did. Old timers say the new arrivals act like they think this is Bethesda. Or is it that Deborah and I are just "an old couple with grandchildren" who seem irrelevant? Prosperous young families have perfect lawns, hybrid electric cars, and husbands who don't wave back when they walk their dogs in their business suits.

My unfashionably unfeminist wife is a founder of a multi-million dollar catering company. The children — Hannah, Peter, and Nicholas — have houses of their own now. Someday, if not already, they'll remember this one's crotchety coziness, its smells, and its slants of light.

This is where we lived. And where we live.

On Henry Allen

A staff writer and editor at *The Washington Post*, 1970-2009, Allen was awarded first prize for commentary by the American Society of Newspaper Editors (1992) and the Pulitzer Prize for criticism (2000). Among his books: *Going Too Far Enough: American Culture at Century's End* (Smithsonian Institution Press), *What It Felt Like: Living in the American Century* (Pantheon), *Fool's Mercy: a novel* (Houghton-Mifflin), and *The Museum of Lost Air: poetry* (Dryad Press). He has written for *The New York Review of Books*, *The New Yorker*, *Paris Review*, *Vogue*, *Wilson Quarterly*, and *The Wall Street Journal*. Allen's been a guest on radio and television, including the Charlie Rose Show, Discovery Channel, NPR's Talk of the Nation, Stephen Colbert, and has given talks in venues at Princeton University, University of Michigan (Graham Hovey Lecture), Pennsylvania State University, American University, and the F. Scott Fitzgerald Literary Festival. He's taught cultural analysis in the University of Maryland honors program. His art (http://henryallenstudio. blogspot. com/) has been shown at the Museum of Contemporary Art (Washington, D.C.), a one-man exhibit at the mansion at Strathmore (North Bethesda, Maryland), and "Celebrating the Hopper Landscape" (Truro, Massachusetts). He lives with his wife Deborah Allen in Takoma Park, Maryland.

WHERE WE LIVED
BY HENRY ALLEN

*is designed by Sandy Rodgers. The text is typeset
in Fournier Standard and the titles in
Fournier Standard Italic.
The book is printed on acid-free papers
by Thomson-Shore.*